BOBBETTE & BELLE

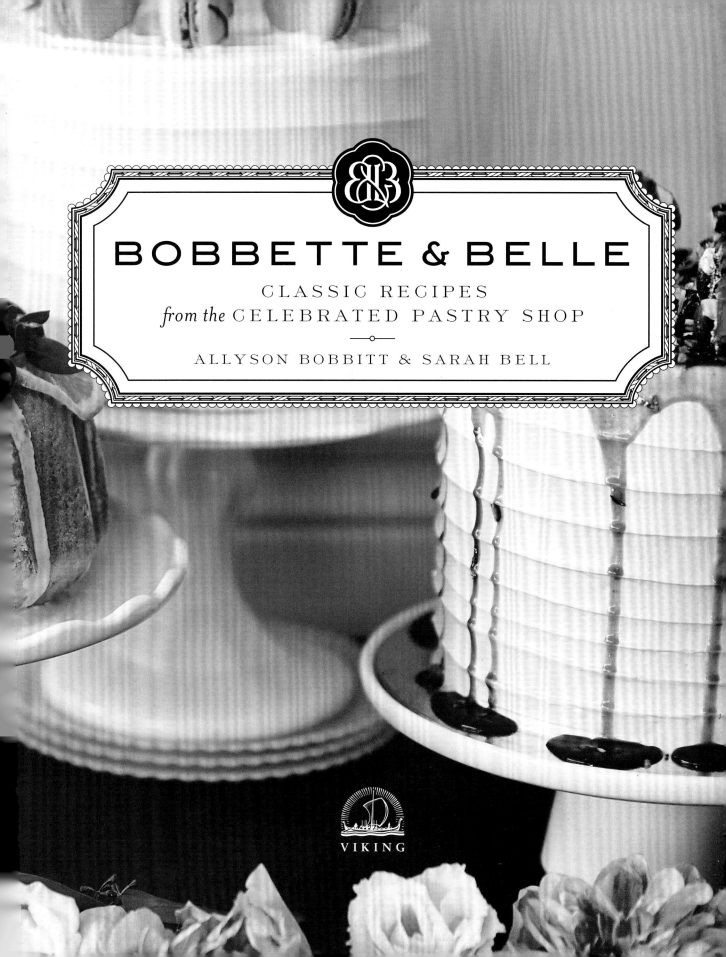

BOBBETTE & BELLE

CLASSIC RECIPES
from the CELEBRATED PASTRY SHOP

ALLYSON BOBBITT & SARAH BELL

VIKING

VIKING

an imprint of Penguin Canada, a division of Penguin Random House Canada Limited

Canada • USA • UK • Ireland • Australia • New Zealand • India • South Africa • China

First published 2016

Photography by Ryan Szulc
Food and prop styling by Allyson Bobbitt and Sarah Bell
Photos of authors on page viii by Malcolm Brown
Photo on page vi–vii by Donna Griffith Photography
Photo on page 149 by Trish Papadakos
Photos on pages 214, 216–217 and 220–221 by Krista Fox Photography

www.penguinrandomhouse.ca

Library and Archives Canada Cataloguing in Publication

Bobbitt, Allyson, author
      Bobbette & Belle : classic recipes from the celebrated
pastry shop / Allyson Bobbitt and Sarah Bell.

ISBN 978-0-670-06832-6 (hardback)
ISBN 978-0-14-319833-8 (electronic)

      1. Pastry. 2. Desserts. 3. Cookbooks I. Bell, Sarah
Kathryn, author II. Title. III. Title: Bobbette and Belle.

TX773.B63 2016   641.86′5   C2015-908752-X

Cover and book design by Chad Roberts and Ian Fotheringham, Chad Roberts Design Ltd.
Cover images by Ryan Szulc

Printed and bound in China

10 9 8 7 6 5 4 3 2 1

Penguin
Random
House

It is difficult to express in words how much the making of a book, or an entire business for that matter, is the result of the combined support, understanding and dedication of the people behind the scenes that help to make our vision possible. We are so thankful to our families, friends and staff for all that they do and are grateful to be able to dedicate this book to them. Nothing we have created thus far or still dream to create in the future would ever be possible without the generous contribution of each and every one of you.

ALLYSON AND SARAH

CONTENTS

THE
BOBBETTE
& BELLE
STORY

We came to our career and passion for pastry in very different ways. Sarah experienced little baking in her home when she was growing up, but her interest was sparked early on by television baking shows and cookbooks. By the end of high school she was convinced that pastry was the only occupation for her. She enrolled in the baking program at George Brown College and from there went on to a pastry job at a high-end restaurant.

In contrast, Allyson's journey to a career in pastry was a bit lengthier. Allyson grew up in a household filled with baking, where her grandmother passed on her skills and knowledge throughout her childhood. Baking was such a part of Allyson's daily life that she never really saw it as a career. All through high school she channelled her creativity into designing, illustrating, sewing or building at every opportunity, but ended up following a more business-minded path and eventually settling into a teaching career. Several years later and still dreaming of being a creative entrepreneur, she stumbled upon an article about the artistry of wedding cakes, and it was a true epiphany. She knew with complete certainty that this was the creative path she was always meant to take.

As it happened, Sarah was experiencing an epiphany of her own. Being the nose-to-the-grindstone person that she is, Sarah had quickly moved from a pastry cook to pastry chef at one of Toronto's top restaurants. It was a wonderful achievement for someone so young, and in many ways it was a dream job. After a couple of years she was at the top of her career, but she was also feeling overwhelmed, exhausted and a bit disillusioned about her future in pastry. She gave her notice and took two jobs, one at a confectionery arts school and another as a chocolatier, while she tried to figure out her next step.

We both attended a class at that school and became casual friends, and we eventually became teachers there too. Allyson spent the next four years building a business designing and making wedding and special-occasion cakes, while Sarah worked and taught at the shop. Once Allyson's business was well established and she was on a high from winning an industry award for top cake designer in Canada, the timing seemed right to expand the business. She had been experimenting with French macarons, then scarcely known in Canada. She knew she would need a partner and immediately thought of Sarah. As it turned out, Sarah had also been experimenting with the macaron in her free time! Our business was born.

We often joke that we are two parts of the same brain, or say that in our case, one plus one equals three. We think of Bobbette & Belle as an extension of ourselves. Every detail—from the tartness of the lemon curd to the texture of a cake to the paint colour, furnishings and decorations in our shops—has been conceived, created or approved by us. We want customers to love our cakes and pastries, of course, but we also want them to love the feeling they get when they come into the shop.

To say the past seven years have been a whirlwind would be an understatement. We have gone from making every macaron ourselves in Allyson's basement while we both had our "other" jobs to having two stores, a full line of products and cakes, forty-five employees, regular baking segments on television and of course writing this book. We once made twenty-four thousand macarons to be packaged and delivered on Valentine's Day—the same day we made our first appearance on *The Marilyn Denis Show*. (It's surprising we could still stand, much less make sense!) It has often been a little crazy and stressful, yet every second has been worth it.

As the saying goes, "It takes a village," and we've been fortunate to have a great group of friends and family who love Bobbette & Belle as much as we do. Before we opened our first shop, Sarah's sister went door to door delivering five thousand "Opening Day" postcards to help get the word out, and our good friend Chris showed up at the shop to help almost every day for the first six months. In those early days when we didn't have much staff, Allyson's dad would sit in the front, and whenever a customer came in, he'd run to the kitchen to let us know so one of us could whip our apron off and go out to serve them!

Last weekend we were getting ready for an annual wedding show. Allyson was building display walls in the loading dock with her compound miter saw, while Sarah, who was nine months pregnant, was packaging hundreds of favours for the show. Meanwhile, our staff in the kitchen started a pool betting on Sarah's due date. We stopped for a moment and took it all in. We work very hard, but we are also very fortunate to do what we love and to have a wonderful team that supports us.

Allyson & Sarah

ESSENTIAL TOOLS & INGREDIENTS

It's been said that "any team is only as strong as its "weakest link" and likewise, any pastry is only as good as the quality of the ingredients used and the knowledge of the tools involved. Fortunately, you don't have to be a pastry chef to acquire the best of both. We are happy to share a few tips and recommendations we have accumulated over the years. They will help you to achieve success with the recipes you try, and most importantly, they will help to make the process truly enjoyable.

ESSENTIAL TOOLS

Coco Chanel once famously said, "Before you leave the house, look in the mirror and take one thing off." Well, as it turns out, the same thing goes for writing a cookbook. We started with a massive list of tools but quickly realized that what we really want to share are the key tools of the trade that consistently make a difference to the quality and ease of baking. Not a tool list, but more like a tool belt. We hope Coco would approve!

STAND MIXER

KitchenAid makes a fantastic stand mixer that we highly recommend. It's a reliable workhorse you can count on again and again.

We have massive commercial mixers at the shops but they still share space with a small regatta of shiny silver KitchenAid stand mixers. If you already own a 5-quart version, it will work wonderfully for our recipes, but if you are thinking of investing in a new one, or trading up, we highly recommend a 7-quart version for larger batches and for ease of use.

CANDY THERMOMETER

Several years ago a friend called in tears after a second failed attempt at making English toffee, swearing that she had definitely used a candy thermometer. We later found out that at the last minute she'd accidentally purchased a meat thermometer from the dollar store. There are many things you can successfully make even if you don't have quite the right tool, but candy is not one of them. A candy thermometer is the last thing on anyone's mind until, well, you want to make candy. Do yourself a favour and buy a good-quality one next time you're at the kitchen store.

BENCH SCRAPER *(dough scraper)*

If there is one tool you never knew you needed that you won't be able to live without, it's a bench scraper. Oddly, we rarely use it for dough, but we find it's a cake-making staple. We prefer stainless steel ones because they are more durable and hold their shape longer, but plastic is fine as well. If you have ever wondered how pastry chefs get their icing so smooth, they use a bench scraper paired with a revolving cake stand to get that professional look a lot easier than they would with a palette knife alone. And we always use a quick swipe of ours to level off dry ingredients in the measuring cup.

PARCHMENT PAPER

The little black dress of kitchen tools, parchment paper is good for almost any occasion. As part of the polyester generation, we grew up with waxed paper, but parchment can do all of those duties and, unlike waxed paper, it's oven-safe. This makes it perfect for lining pans and baking sheets to provide a non-stick surface. Simply trace around your cake pan with pencil, cut out the circle or square and flip it over into the pan (so you don't get any pencil transfer in your cake). It can also be folded quickly into a makeshift piping bag if needed. The uses are almost limitless. It is easy to find in almost any supermarket.

OFFSET ICING SPATULA

Most home bakers are familiar with the standard straight spatula—we mean the long, narrow stainless steel one, not the plastic stirring one—but less so with an offset spatula. With its tilted handle, it's perfect for filling and masking cakes. They come in a variety of sizes, and you can pick some up at the dollar store or kitchen store.

LIQUID AND DRY MEASURING CUPS

It is tempting to use the same set of measuring cups for everything, but we highly recommend having a set of a dry measuring cups and a few different-sized liquid measuring cups. Tempered glass or clear plastic liquid cups allow you to keep the cup level on an even surface as you pour in your ingredient.

In contrast, dry measure cups are opaque because they are meant to be filled and levelled off. Spoon your ingredient into the dry measure and then level it off—we give it one quick swipe with our handy bench scraper (see above). *Do not* knock or bang the cup to level it off, as this can result in compacting the ingredient and therefore using more than the recipe calls for.

PANS

We recommend having on hand a variety of standard-size pans, at minimum a muffin pan, two large baking sheets, three 9-inch round cake pans, an 8- or 9-inch springform pan and a loaf or a Bundt pan (or both!). There is no need to purchase anything fancy. We swear by the inexpensive lightweight aluminum pans you can usually find in your local Chinatown or restaurant supply store—they help cakes bake evenly without over-browning. For non-stick pans, we like the light- and medium-coloured variety for Bundts and tart pans (as you cannot use parchment paper in these pans to prevent sticking). In our experience, the darker charcoal-coloured variety cause items to brown excessively.

REVOLVING CAKE STAND

Many people ice their cakes on a non-moving surface, but it is so much easier and faster to use a revolving cake stand (a.k.a. turntable). Think of a potter's wheel. If you place your cake on the cake stand and rotate it as you spread your icing, it will make for even placement and much less arm strain. Don't spend too much money on a fancy cake-decorating turntable. You can pick up an inexpensive one at Ikea or a discount kitchen store. A useful cake stand should spin easily, stay level with a cake on it and not tilt when pressure is applied. We also like it to be several inches wider than a cake so when you're masking, you can rest the edge of your bench scraper on it, at a 90-degree angle, while you rotate.

FOOD PROCESSOR

Hauling out the food processor can often seem like a hassle, and some people cringe when they see it mentioned in a recipe. But it is truly one of the stars of the kitchen, often called upon to blitz ingredients, combine dough, and coarsely chop nuts and dried fruits. It is equally useful in savoury food prep. Although doughs sometimes require a standard-size model, for many other baking needs you can use a small version. It makes for quick prep and easy cleanup.

COOKIE PORTIONERS

Ice-cream scoops come in about eight different sizes and are incredibly useful for portioning doughs and batters. A larger scoop makes quick work of evenly filling cupcake liners, and smaller versions make perfectly even drop cookies. It's well worth acquiring a few, and they're readily available online.

PIPING BAG AND TIPS

For piping bags and tips, it is worth the time and money to find quality professional brands such as Ateco, Wilton and our favourite, PME. There is nothing worse than piping cookies only to have your piping bag split along the seam. This will virtually never happen with a quality bag. Professional tips come in a wide variety of sizes and shapes and are less likely to rust. Always purchase couplers as well. They make it quick and easy to switch your tips without the hassle of changing bags. (Buy more than one. They get lost so easily, and it is also convenient to be able to prep several colours in several bags if you are piping cookies or cupcakes.)

SILPAT SILICONE MATS

Non-stick silicone baking mats have been used in commercial bakeries for years but have only become available to the general public in the past decade. They fit standard-size baking and cookie sheets and provide a non-stick surface that doesn't require the use of additional fats. They are easy to clean and durable which makes them well worth the expense.

FINE-MESH SIEVE

Sieves come in a variety of weaves. The fine-mesh version, which sometimes has two mesh layers extremely close together, is a great tool for straining the pulp and zest out of curds to achieve a smooth, velvety texture. They are also great for dusting scones and tortes with a light, even layer of icing sugar or cocoa. Simply hold the sieve a couple of feet above the pastry and gently tap it to distribute the sugar or cocoa. Spend a few extra dollars on quality: with cheaper ones, handles can bend or break and the mesh tears easily.

ESSENTIAL INGREDIENTS
That Make a Difference

There are lots of ingredients that, despite their fancy brand names and packaging, are almost identical to their no-name counterparts. However, there is also a small selection of ingredients for which we can accept no substitutions. Whether the ingredient is more expensive, harder to source or a favourite staple, these ten are worth using and will noticeably improve your baking results.

UNSALTED BUTTER

There is room for butter and pastry in a balanced diet. It can be tempting to switch out full-fat butter for a less calorie-dense ingredient, but we urge you not to. The fat in butter is unique, in that it adds unparalleled flavour while having the solid structure that most baked goods require. The moisture content in low-fat butter makes it unsuitable for baking, and most butter substitutes are either too soft (such as tub margarine) or contain high levels of trans fat to maintain a solid form (shortening). Always choose unsalted butter, as it lets you control the amount of added salt in a recipe, allowing for the best balance of flavours.

HIGH QUALITY CHOCOLATE

We can't say enough how important it is to use high-quality chocolate. It doesn't have to be outrageously expensive, and you'll find wonderful brands at a reasonable price, including Lindt and Callebaut. Avoid "baking" chocolates, which often have an off-putting waxy texture.

DARK DUTCH PROCESSED COCOA

Growing up, there seemed to be only one type of cocoa, but in fact, like chocolate, not all cocoas are created equal. We have done side-by-side test bakes with different varieties, and you would be surprised by the difference quality makes. It may take a bit of searching to find the best quality dark cocoa you can. Sometimes it is available in bulk and other times it may only be found at specialty food stores.

CREAM CHEESE

Thankfully, Philadelphia-brand cream cheese is available in a 50-pound commercial size or we would be unwrapping a lot of those small silver packages at our shops! With a lot of ingredients it doesn't matter which brand you use, but in this case we recommend buying Philadelphia. It seems to be creamier and less wet than other brands, even when the moisture content is listed as being the same. This may not make a huge difference when it's used as an addition to cakes or loaves, but it makes a big difference in cream cheese buttercream, frostings and cheesecakes. Use the full-fat variety, not "light" ones.

FOOD COLOURING *(professional grade)*

Yes, we know the box says you can mix any colour with just those four little teardrop-shaped bottles, but if you're like us, you've found out the hard way—you can't. They are great for quick basic colouring, but to produce refined-looking macarons, piped cookies and cakes, it is best to look for professional gel food colours (also known as pastes). The good news is, they can often be found at craft and bulk food stores. Look for professional-grade brands such as Wilton, Americolor and Sugarflair. Colours like ivory are a must, as they can quickly temper brighter colours or shades that look too childish. We recommend getting a good bright red, a lavender, a soft pink, a yellow-based green like avocado, a sky blue and a lemon yellow. This selection will truly give you a multitude of mixing options.

NUTS

If you have ever bitten into a rancid nut, you know exactly what we are going to say. There is nothing worse than taking the time to bake something from scratch only to have it ruined by the overpowering flavour of less-than-fresh nuts. In our experience, packaged nuts from the grocery store can be of unreliable freshness, and more often than not they're rancid. While we don't condone excessive tasting of unpurchased nuts, we do recommend buying nuts at a shop that has high turnover and where you can test one or two. Nuts are an expensive ingredient, and it's nice to know what you're getting.

FULL-FAT DAIRY

Using light sour cream, yogurt or milk makes little difference to the calorie count of many recipes, but it makes a huge difference to the taste and texture. Even small differences in the ratio of fat to dry ingredients can alter recipe results. In recipes created to be low calorie, the reduction in fat is compensated for by the addition of liquids or fruit purées. Such recipes have been specifically formulated with these changes in mind. For the best results with our recipes, we highly recommend that you use only full-fat dairy.

FRUIT *(high-quality purées, seasonal fresh or frozen)*

We did not group our recipes by season, but we do recommend that when you're choosing a fruit recipe to make, you give some thought to what is seasonally available. If a recipe calls for fresh fruit, we recommend either making that recipe when the fruit is in season or substituting fruits that are currently in season. In several cases, like our Quick and Easy Summer Fruit Torte, we suggest alternative fruit combinations that will work in different seasons. In-season fruits are often better quality and may even be grown locally, which, in our opinion, typically results in better flavour. If a recipe calls for frozen fruit, of course it can be made at any time of the year. If it calls for fruit purées, you can purée frozen fruit or use a quality store-bought fruit purée.

PURE MAPLE SYRUP

Take a moment to enjoy the rosy glow of national pride. If France is known for butter, we are known for amazing maple syrup. In fact, each year Canada produces more than 80 percent of the world's pure maple syrup. A light amber syrup is sufficient for dowsing pancakes and waffles, but for baking you want the more intense maple flavour that comes from Grade A dark or amber syrups.

PURE MADAGASCAR BOURBON VANILLA

Vanilla is without a doubt the most expensive ingredient in baking. However, a little goes a long way, and it is worth the investment to purchase a pure vanilla extract like those made by Nielsen-Massey. The difference in depth of flavour is striking and can make or break desserts that feature vanilla, such as panna cotta, vanilla cake and crème brûlée.

GENERAL BAKING TIPS

There is an overwhelming array of baking tips and tricks that we could share, but we have chosen to focus on some key points that are easy to incorporate, and will make a big difference to your baking results. These are also tips that are often forgotten or rushed through, so we wanted to stress their importance and give some explanations for why we think they are worth the extra effort to incorporate.

GENERAL BAKING TIPS

MISE EN PLACE

It is appropriate to start with the importance of mise en place, which is French for "putting in place," or as we like to say, "a stich is time saves nine." Professional chefs are fanatical about mise en place because in a commercial kitchen, timing and limiting the number of times you have to switch tasks are the only paths to accomplishing all that has to get done in a day. At home it sometimes feels easier to dive in and measure and chop as you go along, but we cannot say enough about how much more enjoyable your baking experience will be, how much more intuitive it feels and how much more success you will achieve if you take 10 minutes to read over the entire recipe as well as prep and measure all the ingredients before you start to bake. The funny thing is, this more mindful approach always ends up saving time in the end. We like to think of it as the Zen of Baking.

GRATE YOUR BUTTER

When making pie crusts and doughs, you need to be able to work in cold butter so that the pieces are neither too big nor too fine. We recommend using the large holes of a box grater to grate cold butter into coarse pieces that can be easily incorporated into the flour mixture without overworking the butter or the dough.

USE ROOM-TEMPERATURE EGGS

Who remembers to take the eggs out of the fridge 30 minutes before baking a cake? Very few of us, which is why it is so tempting to skip this step, but we advise you not to for a couple of really good reasons. First, you are often instructed to add eggs after creaming your room-temperature butter and sugar. If you add cold eggs to this creamed mixture, the fat in the butter will start to harden, resulting in a curdled appearance and a reduction in fluffiness. Second, if you are making a meringue and use cold egg whites instead of room-temperature ones, the meringue will have less volume and be significantly less fluffy.

If you do forget to take the eggs out of the fridge, simply let them sit in a bowl of warm water for 10 minutes while you measure your other ingredients and prepare your pans.

USE AN OVEN THERMOMETER

Individual oven temperatures vary. Making sure your oven is the correct temperature can really make a difference to the final product. For instance, scones benefit greatly from being baked at a higher heat, and their taste and texture would suffer if they were baked lower and slower. In contrast, shortbread likes to be baked low and slow and would over-brown at a higher temperature.

This is where a good-quality oven thermometer is a wise investment. Place the thermometer on the middle oven rack and set your oven to 350°F. Once the oven comes up to heat, check the thermometer at least twice, about 15 minutes apart, to allow for on/off cycling. If it reads 350°F, your baking times should be close to ours. If it reads lower or higher, adjust your oven setting up or down in 25°F increments until your thermometer reads 350°F. Once you know by how much your oven is off, you can calibrate the oven's thermostat—or always remember to adjust the temperature up or down from what is stated in the recipe.

MAKE FRIENDS WITH YOUR OVEN

Oven temperatures can vary significantly between the top and the bottom, and many ovens have hot spots, so it is always good to get to know your own oven. Our oven is like a trusted friend: we know its strengths and its weaknesses and we adjust accordingly. Get to know your oven in the same way. If a recipe specifies to bake on the middle rack but the bottoms of your cakes always come out too dark while the tops are just baked, your oven's sweet spot may be the rack above the middle. Once you know your oven, you'll be able to confidently ignore the recipe, knowing it means better baking results.

TOAST NUTS AND COCONUT

Preheat your oven to 350°F. Line a baking sheet with parchment paper and sprinkle the nuts or shredded coconut in an even layer on the tray. Toast nuts in the oven for 8 to 10 minutes or coconut for 5 to 7 minutes. Check often to ensure that the nuts or coconut do not burn, and rotate the baking sheet halfway through to ensure even toasting. Once the nuts or coconut are a light golden colour and their aroma fills the room, remove from the oven and leave to cool completely before using.

After toasting hazelnuts, remove the skins by wrapping the cooled nuts in a tea towel. On a hard surface, rub the towel with the nuts in it back and forth. The friction will loosen the skins. Continue with this motion until most of the skins are removed. Some skins will remain. Pick out the hazelnuts and discard the skins.

DO NOT OVERMIX

We asked friends and family to test-bake our recipes at home to make sure we were giving readers enough information, to check that the recipes work in a home oven, and to see how similar the results were to ours. The most significant differences in the results came from our test bakers' interpretation of the phrases "do not overmix" and "mix until just combined." Overmixing leads to tough and dense cakes and cookies, and to "tunnelling" in the finished product. As a result, we have provided as many specific mixing times as possible. You might see mixing time as free time in which to get other things prepped, but mixing time should always be monitored. Add ingredients and mix. When everything just comes together, stop the mixer and scrape down the sides of the bowl, then very briefly mix to properly incorporate any bottom and side bits you have just loosened.

THOROUGHLY CLEAN & DRY YOUR BOWL

Before you whip egg whites for any preparation, whether a cake, pavlova or royal icing, make sure the bowl is completely free from any kind of fat residue. A meringue will fail or a royal icing will not dry properly if some fats have accidentally made their way in. A basic dish detergent is excellent at removing grease. If you do notice that your meringue is falling a bit flat, quit while you're ahead and start over. Recipes calling for meringue usually require you to beat the whites as a separate step, which allows for a second chance if something goes awry.

LINE PANS WITH PARCHMENT PAPER

You don't *have* to line pans with parchment paper, but in our experience it results in faster cleanup and virtually guarantees that your baked goods will not stick to the pan. To this day we still cut out individual circles of parchment for every layer of cake we bake. That can mean cutting more than 200 circles a day, but it's worth it to ensure a consistent result. (We could buy pre-cut rounds, but they're way more expensive, and we find that a variety of sizes are easier to cut from one large sheet.)

ROTATE YOUR PANS

Oven temperatures vary between racks. When you're baking on one rack, usually the middle, rotate the pans front to back midway through baking. If you're baking on several racks at the same time, rotate the pans front to back and top to bottom. This simple task will help to ensure even baking. Be sure to allow items to bake for at least half their total bake time before you rotate them. For items like cakes that need to rise during baking, rotating before the batter has set can cause it to deflate and result in a slumped centre.

JUST FAIL BETTER

We're firm believers in the famous slogan "Just do it," but since it sometimes seems to imply "just do it right," we've added another motivational phrase: "Just fail better." If it comes out perfectly, great, but if it doesn't, it probably still tastes pretty darn good and it will always get you one step closer to success the next time. We baked what we jokingly refer to as "maca-wrongs" for six months before we could consistently bake great French macarons. Trust us, we shed more than a few late-night tears over failed batches, but there were also plenty of times we chopped up those maca-wrongs and ate them on top of ice cream, proving that sometimes a couple of maca-wrongs do make a right.

TIPS
FOR
SPECIFIC
PASTRIES

We've already provided some general tips and tricks that will be useful for all sorts of baking, but you may find yourself challenged by baking a specific type of pastry. Most pastry recipes are formed from a small number of key ingredients, yet because of the particular methodology used to create each type of pastry, there's an immense range in the resulting textures, flavours and varieties. The eggs, almond flour and sugar that provide the base for a dense almond torte are the same ingredients that, when manipulated differently, result in an impossibly light and airy macaron shell. Because each method has such a profound impact on the end result, here we list some of the key tips for preparing different types of pastry. We hope they will help you bake with confidence and give you the skills to begin problem solving if something doesn't seem quite right.

FRENCH MACARONS

Perhaps more than any other sweet, barring chocolate, making French macarons requires passion, an inquisitive mind and more than a touch of patience. It is best to think of it as a project rather than a recipe, as failure is often the only path to a successful macaron. Rather than being a negative thing, the challenge has always confirmed for us that baking truly is a science, and rather than being constraining, the challenge gives us the freedom to experiment. One of the most satisfying things about baking is being able to see how even the smallest change can make an impact, often for the better.

DEFINING THE PRIZE

A well-executed macaron consists of a smooth, glossy shell that is a bit crisp but gives way to a soft, slightly chewy centre. It should have a "lacy foot" that runs evenly around the entire base of the shell and be as consistent in size as possible. It may seem daunting, but each of these features provides a hint of what may be tweaked or adjusted in order to achieve success.

IN SEARCH OF A SMOOTH SHELL

When you start out, a smooth, glossy macaron shell can seem as elusive as a unicorn.

• Store brands of almond flour (also known as almond meal) can be quite coarse, which will give unwanted texture to your baked shell. You want to use a fine flour. It may seem intuitive to toss it in a food processor, but we advise against this unless you really, really like almond butter. Instead, pass the ground almonds through a fine sieve and discard any larger pieces. Then sift together your almond flour and the icing sugar the recipe calls for. This second sifting makes a big difference.

• Once you have piped your shells, give the trays several even bangs on the counter to smooth out the tops and get rid of any marks left by the piping tip. If your macarons look more like a kiss and won't even out, it is likely that the meringue was a bit too stiff. Reduce your whisking time the next time. It may also be the case that the almond and meringue mixture needed to be folded together a little longer to loosen up.

• If your baked shells look transparent or marbled, you may have over-folded the meringue when incorporating it into the almond flour. It should be well combined and have the look of molten lava. Folding beyond this point will result in a mottled appearance and an internal air pocket.

CRISP YET SOFT: ACHIEVING THE PERFECT MOUTH FEEL

A macaron has a meringue base that allows it to form a crisp outer shell while maintaining a soft, slightly chewy centre.

• Once piped, the shells need to rest to form an outer skin. The length of time often varies by temperature and humidity, so it is a good idea to get to know the right texture by feel alone. If you gently touch the top, a perfect piped meringue should feel dry and not sticky, but if you apply any pressure, it should still feel quite soft underneath. In your first attempts, try letting one tray rest longer than the other so you can see the difference an additional 10 minutes can make.

• One thing that helps form the skin is using "aged" egg whites. Aging whites reduces their water content while preserving the protein bonds that help make a stable meringue. This is one of the reasons we don't recommend using packaged liquid egg whites, which are significantly wetter. In France, whites are sometimes aged for several days at room temperature, but we prefer to encourage North American food safety practices. Age your egg whites uncovered at room temperature for 2 hours, then hold the bottom of the bowl in lukewarm water for a minute to warm the whites slightly before using. Be careful not to get any water in the whites.

THE ILLUSTRIOUS "LACY FOOT"

Perhaps the thing that most defines a successful macaron is its lacy foot. The quality of the foot is like the difference between simply passing versus making the honour roll. The goal is to have it perfectly encircle the base, be of uniform height and not be over-inflated or puffy. It sounds picky, but the foot literally forms a map of the entire baking process.

• If your shells dry too long after being piped, or not long enough, they won't form a foot. If this happens, adjust the wait time up or down.

• If it is too humid, or not humid enough, the shells will form what we call a topsy-turvy foot—one that is not uniform. We use humidifiers and dehumidifiers to achieve the perfect level of humidity at the shops, but every time the seasons change we go through several days of testing and tweaking to get back on track. It is nothing less than an art, but in many ways that's the fun part. Try not to bake macarons on rainy days, and turn on the air conditioner in the summer or the humidifier in the winter.

• If the oven temperature is too hot, the foot will quickly over-inflate and end up large and bulbous. If the shells are removed from the oven too soon, before the shell has fully set, the foot will deflate, flatten and extend far beyond the top. Use the oven thermometer test we describe on page 12 to be sure that you are baking at the correct temperature (despite what your oven says).

• Test if the macarons are done by gently pressing on a top. If it jiggles, they need a bit more time. If it is set and doesn't move easily, they are ready to be removed from the oven. If you find your macaron tops are browning, reduce the temperature next time or bake only on the lower rack of the oven.

CAKES & CUPCAKES

We make many different types of pastry at our shops, but Bobbette & Belle is perhaps best known for our cakes and cupcakes. Before we opened, we were both struck by how often we would pick up a delicious-looking pastry or slice of cake somewhere, only to be disappointed by the taste. We didn't want to reinvent the wheel; we just wanted to bake cakes from scratch with high-quality ingredients and an eye for detail. We wanted to take people by surprise when they remember, with the first bite, how great cake can actually taste. It is easy to bake a cake, but is difficult to bake a really great cake, so we're providing some of our tips and secrets to help you along.

LET THERE BE CAKE

There are three main types of cake batters: chiffon, which involves folding a meringue into your batter to add lightness; oil-based, which is often the easiest method and typically used for cakes requiring a particularly moist base, such as chocolate, red velvet and carrot; and creaming-method batters, in which sugar and butter are creamed together until light and fluffy before other ingredients are added. Vanilla cakes, which often require a lighter crumb and buttery flavour, tend to start with the creaming method.

DON'T FORGET TO WARM UP

Always use room-temperature eggs, milk and butter. This is one of those steps that is tempting to skip, but it really does make a difference to the final texture of the cake. Your batter will be lighter and fluffier and require less mixing if you give your ingredients time to come to room temperature.

FLUFF IT UP

When creaming your butter and sugar, you need to cream for an adequate amount of time to achieve a light texture, otherwise your cake will be dense. The creamed mixture should be light and fluffy and very light in colour. Typically this takes at least a full 3 minutes at medium-high speed with a stand mixer, longer with a handheld electric beater.

TAKING TURNS

Many recipes direct you to alternate adding the flour and liquids in three parts, always beginning and ending with flour. It is very easy to forget to do this or reverse the order of additions. We recommend sticking to what is specified in each recipe, as the correct order of additions will lead to a smoother batter with fewer lumps and as a result require less mixing.

MIX MASTER

We mentioned not overmixing in our general tips, but we want to stress it again here because overmixing a cake batter will result in a cake or cupcake that is too dense and not tender. It's important to mix ingredients until fully combined but no further. It's also important to stop the mixer and scrape down the sides and bottom of the bowl, then *briefly* mix to ensure that no unmixed ingredients remain. Any unincorporated clumps of butter and sugar will form holes, craters or large tunnels in the cake as it bakes.

THE PERFECT LAYER

It may be tempting to bake a layer cake in one tall pan rather than two or three separate pans, but we find baking layers individually always yields a better result. At the shops we bake each layer separately to ensure that the finished cake will be uniformly tender and moist. Baking in one large pan causes the outside of the cake to dry out and darken before the centre is properly baked. We also love that baking in individual layers reduces baking time and makes levelling off the finished cake layers much easier. Oh, and don't forget to give your pans a tap or two on the counter before baking to release extra air bubbles.

ON THE RISE

When preparing a cake batter, once the liquid portion has been added to the dry ingredients, the leavening agents, such as baking soda or baking powder, will be activated. It is important to get the batter in the oven as soon as possible, as any additional sitting time may over-activate the leaveners to the point of exhaustion, resulting in a dense cake.

UP, DOWN AND ALL AROUND

We can't stress enough how important it is to rotate your pans back to front and up and down for even baking. Remember not to rotate until the batter has baked enough to set, typically halfway through the baking time, or it will lose volume when moved. Rotating also helps cake layers stay even, so there is less trimming before assembly.

ON THE LEVEL

At Bobbette & Belle, our cakes are known for their extremely even and flat layers. Freshly baked cake that has cooled to room temperature is often soft and unwieldy, making it difficult to trim, fill and mask. We recommend chilling the cake layers for an hour or so before trimming and filling.

PUT IT ON ICE

If you've baked your cake or cupcakes but are not planning to assemble them for several days or longer, you can wrap the layers individually in plastic wrap and then a layer of tin foil and freeze until ready to use. For cupcakes, we recommend that you layer them in an airtight container with a piece of parchment paper between the layers. Cake layers and cupcakes can be frozen for up to one month. Unwrapped cake layers will thaw at room temperature in an hour or so.

DELAYED GRATIFICATION

Storing cakes in the fridge will extend their shelf life so you can enjoy them longer, but always allow the cake or slice to return to room temperature before serving. The butter in buttercream and frosting hardens when refrigerated and needs to warm up to become light and fluffy again.

PASTRY DOUGH

Pie doughs and tart crusts can seem daunting. After all, most of us have tasted a crust that looked great but was disappointingly tough and flavourless. It is particularly tricky to make a flaky crust without the addition of shortening, which we don't use because of the concern about its high trans fat content. The good news is, a delicious buttery tender crust is within reach. We've listed some of our favourite tips and general info that will make pie and tart making a piece of cake, so to speak.

THE BIG CHILL
Unlike cake batters, pie and tart doughs require cold ingredients. Not just butter, but even cold flour and ice water.

THE GRATER GOOD
As we mentioned on page 12, use a grater to coarsely grate your cold butter so it can be more easily mixed through with the flour. This will result in less manipulation of the dough and help prevent toughness.

A GENTLE TOUCH
Use delicate hands. Pie crust, tart dough and scone dough require a particularly delicate approach. It is tempting to overwork the dough, as it is intuitive to think of doughs as requiring kneading, but unlike bread doughs, tart, pie and scone dough should be manipulated only until the ingredients come together. Even then, it is fine, and in fact desirable, to see some small pieces of butter that are not fully incorporated. These specks of butter melt in the oven and create the small layers of air that give pastry a light, flaky texture.

GET SOME REST
To help avoid shrinkage and toughness, allow your dough to rest for the recommended length of time when it is first made and then again once you have lined the tart or pie pan. Any time dough is worked, no matter how gently, it develops toughening gluten. Letting it rest relaxes the gluten.

KEEP ON ROLLING
To easily transfer the dough into your tart pan or pie dish, roll the dough onto your rolling pin and then unroll it over the pan.

BE PREPARED FOR SHRINKAGE
Be sure to leave a little extra dough at the top of the tart pan or pie dish to accommodate any shrinkage that might occur during baking.

CAN'T TAKE THE HEAT
Often the edges of the crust take on too much colour before the bottom of the crust is fully baked. To prevent overbaking, cover the edges with a ring of tin foil three-quarters of the way through baking.

WEIGHTY ISSUES
If you are pre-baking your crust, it must first be "docked" and weighted down to prevent large air bubbles from forming in the pastry. To dock the crust, prick the entire bottom of the crust with a fork, being very careful to score the top but not fully pierce through to the bottom, or else your filling will leak into the baked pastry, making it soggy. Place a large piece of parchment on top of the dough and fill it with 1 to 2 cups of dried beans to weigh it down. The beans can easily be removed after baking and can be reused (but make sure you don't cook with them!).

COOKIES & CONFECTIONS

For most of us, making cookies was our first experience with baking. In fact, several of the cookie recipes we use in our shops as well as in this book were directly transcribed from the original handwritten recipe cards from our childhood. Cookies never fail to be addictive, and making them is straightforward and easy once you know a few key tips.

PREP YOUR PANS

Line your baking sheets with parchment paper or silicone baking for a non-stick surface that is quick and easy to clean up.

THE CREAMING METHOD

The first step in most cookie recipes is to blend the butter and sugar in a mixer. Allow more time than you think for this step, about 3 full minutes or until the mixture is light and fluffy and very pale in colour. As in any baking, be sure to start with room-temperature butter, but make sure it's not too soft or the cookies will spread and flatten excessively during baking.

JUST THE RIGHT MIX

At the risk of sounding repetitive, be careful not to overmix. Just like cakes and pie crusts, cookies can become tough and hard if they are overmixed once the flour has been added. Make sure to scrape down the sides and bottom of the bowl so everything is incorporated, but otherwise mix only until all the ingredients have come together.

PORTION CONTROLLED

Use a small portioning scoop to make sure that your cookies are all close to the same size. Even small differences can lead to some cookies being overbaked while others on the same sheet are under-baked.

GIVE IT A REST

Rolled cookie doughs for sugar cookies and shortbread are a lot like pie doughs. They have to be handled gently and they need chilling time in the fridge to let the gluten strands relax. If you can chill the rolled-out dough, that is best, as it will make the dough easier to cut and help the cookies retain their shape in the oven.

THE DEEP FREEZE

Doughs for rolled and drop cookies can be frozen for later use. Cookie dough that's to be rolled should be shaped into several discs; wrap each in plastic wrap and freeze in a freezer bag. Portion drop cookie dough, roll into balls and place on a baking sheet. Refrigerate until well chilled (to prevent sticking), then transfer to an airtight container and freeze for up to 1 month.

KEEP IT CLEAN

When making candy such as toffee and other confections, it is imperative that your bowl and tools be very clean with no fat or other residue. Any accidental contaminants will cause the sugar to crystallize.

TEMPERATURE TAKING

Be sure to use a candy thermometer when making confections such as toffee. Even a few degrees above or below the right temperature can lead to toffee that is either too soft and chewy or so hard you may need to see your dentist.

ALTERNATIVE BAKING
& DIETARY RESTRICTIONS

We will be the first to say that this is not an alternative baking book, and we are certainly not experts in this area. That being said, however, we have always found it a shame that many people are unable to fully enjoy traditional baking books because of dietary restrictions. Over the years many of our customers have told us that they wish they could enjoy more of our baked goods but they are unable to eat gluten, dairy or both. In response, we developed an alternative flour blend that can be used in place of wheat flour in many of our recipes, and in this section we also suggest some dairy replacements, including for butter. At the shops, we are able to customize many of our cakes using our flour substitute, and it is next to impossible to tell the difference between them and our regular cakes.

GLUTEN SUBSTITUTES

For those with a gluten sensitivity or celiac disease, gluten causes a whole host of problems, ranging from minor discomfort to serious illness. For pastry chefs, there is a long tradition of using wheat flour because it so easily produces a wide variety of baked goods. Unfortunately, the wheat proteins that cause so much distress in those who are intolerant are the very components that make wheat flour the best choice for baking. Wheat proteins provide the structure and elasticity that most recipes require. Think of a soft piece of freshly baked bread. It is light and airy while also having a slightly chewy texture.

Because no other single flour variety is able to produce these characteristics, we use a blend of flours in our alternative recipe, achieving each of these qualities with a different flour substitute. The white and brown rice flours provide proteins for structure, the potato starch helps to achieve lightness, while the tapioca starch lends a slight chew. Xanthan gum, which is naturally derived, is the secret weapon, providing both structure and elasticity. Together these ingredients do a great job of mimicking wheat flour, and can be switched out 1 for 1 with wheat flour in many recipes.

We recommend trying this blend in our cake recipes, loaves and Bundts. Because of the importance of gluten to the texture and structure of pie and bread doughs, replacement flour blends are not as successful in these recipes (recipes that use them have to be specifically formulated). If you don't have time to make your own flour blend, we recommend gluten-free flour blends by President's Choice and Bob's Red Mill.

GLUTEN FREE FLOUR BLEND

MAKES ABOUT 8½ CUPS

4½ cups white rice flour

2 cups brown rice flour

1⅓ cups potato starch

¾ cup tapioca starch (tapioca flour)

4½ teaspoons xanthan gum

Tip

Be sure to use potato starch, not potato flour. They are not the same and therefore are not interchangeable. Potato starch adds lightness, whereas potato flour would make baked goods dense and gummy.

1. Measure each ingredient into a large bowl. When measuring the ingredients, do not tap or pack them into the measuring cup. Just spoon in and level off with a knife or bench scraper. Whisk together well.

2. Store in an airtight container in the fridge for up to 3 months.

3. Replace 1 for 1 with the all-purpose flour in a recipe.

DAIRY SUBSTITUTES

Good dairy alternatives are plentiful, but when replacing dairy in baked goods, it is necessary to use substitutes that have a similar texture, fat content, neutral flavour and acid content to cow's milk. For those who can't tolerate butter, the challenge can be finding replacements that don't contain too many additives, preservatives or trans fats. Below are the substitutions that we find work well in place of cow's milk, yogurt, sour cream and butter.

SOY MILK AND YOGURT

Look for plain, unsweetened varieties that are neutral in flavour. The following replacements may be substituted 1 for 1 with dairy in many recipes. We do not recommend dairy substitutes in recipes such as crème brûlée and panna cotta where the feature ingredient is cream.

MILK

We recommend using plain (but not "light") soy milk. It is the closest substitute to regular milk and results in similar texture and consistency in baking.

BUTTERMILK

Some recipes call for buttermilk because its acid content boosts leavening power, which results in lighter and fluffier cakes and muffins. Soy milk can easily replace buttermilk. Simply add 1 tablespoon of an acid such as white vinegar (or lemon juice in a pinch) to "sour" 1 cup of soy milk.

YOGURT AND SOUR CREAM

Yogurt and sour cream are used in baking to provide moisture and produce a more tender crumb in cakes, muffins and quick breads. Unsweetened plain 2% to 5% soy yogurt is a great replacement for both.

GHEE AND CLARIFIED BUTTER
as Substitutes for Regular Butter

Butter is a difficult ingredient to replace, as very few alternatives work like it in baking. Butter's delicious yet neutral flavour, as well as its solid form, make it perfect for a wide variety of recipes.

One store-bought butter substitute that has worked for us in baking is Earth Balance Vegan Shortening Sticks (trans fat free).

This product works great as a general butter substitute, but we would not recommend it for recipes where butter is the focus, like a Swiss meringue buttercream. If you are looking for a dairy-free frosting, buttercream or filling substitute, many store-bought frosting brands are dairy free.

Another butter substitute we've had success with is ghee. It is very popular in South Asian cuisines for its slightly nutty taste, high smoking point and long shelf life. Ghee is made by heating unsalted butter until the milk solids (which contain lactose) sink to the bottom and brown. The foam from the moisture content is skimmed off the top, and then the pure butterfat is poured off, leaving the solids behind. Ghee is very similar to clarified butter, except that it is cooked longer to caramelize slightly. This requires a more advanced technique, so we recommend purchasing it. You can easily find it in the international or ethnic food aisle of most grocery stores. For more natural colour and flavour, be sure to buy a good-quality one that doesn't contain turmeric or salt.

The recipe below explains how to make your own clarified butter at home, which is quite simple, and it may be used in the same way as ghee.

Ghee and clarified butter do have a different consistency from butter, so, depending how they are used in a recipe, they will quite likely change the final result. For instance, in a pie crust, the water that is trapped in butter turns to steam, causing that wonderful flakiness. But because ghee and clarified butter don't contain water, a pie crust made with either will be oily and dense. It will take some experimenting to find the right recipes in which these substitutes work best. We have had success using a 1 for 1 substitution of either in our cake, cupcake, loaf and Bundt batters.

MAKES ABOUT 1¾ CUPS

1 pound unsalted butter

Tip

Clarified butter is very shelf stable because all the moisture and milk solids (which cause butter to go rancid) have been removed. It can be kept at room temperature in an airtight container for a couple of months or for up to a year in the fridge.

To prevent contamination of your ghee, only use very clean utensils when portioning from the container.

1. Place the butter in a heavy saucepan. Over low heat, and without stirring, melt the butter and cook until bubbling. Let simmer until the foam rises to the top and the solids sink to the bottom and become golden. Watch carefully so that the milk solids don't burn.

2. Remove from the heat and skim off any foam with a spoon. Set a fine-mesh sieve over a heatproof container and line it with a few layers of cheesecloth. Carefully pour the hot butter through the sieve, leaving behind the solids at the bottom of the pot.

3. Let the clarified butter cool to room temperature before storing in an airtight container in the fridge.

1

CLASSIC
COOKIES
AND BARS

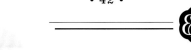

ULTIMATE CHOCOLATE CHIP COOKIES

Chocolate chip is the quintessential North American drop cookie, yet no two recipes are alike. Oats or no oats, chocolate chunks or chocolate chips, white sugar or brown sugar? The varieties are endless and the recipes plentiful, but we are happy to share the recipe for what we consider the ultimate chocolate chip cookie. It is packed with lots of dark chocolate chips, and the oats and brown sugar add depth of flavour and a chewy texture. The result is a buttery, decadent melt-in-your-mouth classic.

1 cup all-purpose flour

1 teaspoon baking powder

1 teaspoon baking soda

½ teaspoon salt

1 cup unsalted butter, room temperature but not soft

½ cup granulated sugar

½ cup loosely packed brown sugar

1 large egg

1 teaspoon pure vanilla extract

2 cups large-flake rolled oats

¾ cup dark chocolate chips

Tip

This recipe is particularly sensitive to the temperature of the butter. It needs to be room temperature but not too soft. If your kitchen is warm, use the butter before it reaches room temperature.

1. Put oven racks in the upper and lower thirds of the oven and preheat the oven to 350°F. Line 2 baking sheets with parchment paper.

2. In a small bowl, whisk together the flour, baking powder, baking soda and salt.

3. In the bowl of a stand mixer fitted with the paddle attachment, cream the butter, granulated sugar and brown sugar on medium speed until light and fluffy, about 3 minutes. Add the egg and vanilla and beat just to combine.

4. With the mixer on low speed, slowly add the flour mixture to the creamed butter mixture, mixing until just combined and scraping down the sides of the bowl at least once. Add the oats and chocolate chips and mix until fully incorporated.

5. Spoon 12 heaping tablespoons of cookie dough onto each lined baking sheet, leaving ample space between them.

6. Bake for 8 to 12 minutes or until the cookies are light golden brown on the bottom. For even baking, rotate the sheets front to back and top to bottom halfway through. Allow the cookies to cool slightly on the baking sheets before transferring them to a wire rack to cool completely. The cookies can be stored in an airtight container for up to 2 weeks.

DOUBLE CHOCOLATE FLEUR DE SEL COOKIES

This is the top-selling cookie at our shops, owing in part to the intensely dark chocolate flavour but also to the contrasting texture and taste of the fleur de sel garnish on top. Salty-sweet combinations have been very popular in the past few years, but the addition of fleur de sel to sweets is a longstanding tradition in French pastry. Salt enhances flavour, and this is particularly true when it's paired with dark chocolate. Fleur de sel de Guérande, which is often considered one of the best salts in the world, is a variety of sea salt harvested in coastal Brittany. Its subtle crunch and delicate flavour make it the perfect choice for a garnish in this recipe, and it is well worth the price tag if you are able to find it.

1¾ cups all-purpose flour

⅓ cup cocoa powder

¾ teaspoon baking soda

¾ teaspoon fleur de sel

1 cup unsalted butter, room temperature

¾ cup loosely packed brown sugar

⅓ cup granulated sugar

1¼ cups dark chocolate chips

1 tablespoon fleur de sel (approx.), for garnish

Tip

There is no need to chill this dough, as it scoops and bakes best at room temperature.

To avoid garnishing with too much fleur de sel, hold your hand about a foot above the cookies and allow the salt to fall evenly.

1. Put oven racks in the upper and lower thirds of the oven and preheat the oven to 350°F. Line 2 baking sheets with parchment paper.

2. In a medium bowl, whisk together the flour, cocoa powder, baking soda and ³⁄₄ teaspoon of the fleur de sel.

3. In the bowl of a stand mixer fitted with a paddle attachment, cream the butter, brown sugar and granulated sugar on medium speed until light and fluffy, about 3 minutes.

4. With the mixer on low speed, slowly add the flour mixture to the creamed butter mixture, mixing until just combined. Add the chocolate chips and continue to mix until fully incorporated, scraping down the sides of the bowl at least once.

5. Roll the cookie dough into 1-inch balls using your hands or use an ice-cream scoop to portion the dough. Arrange 24 balls on each lined baking sheet, leaving ample space between them. Gently press the balls with the bottom of a cup until they are approximately ¹⁄₂-inch thick.

6. Bake for 12 to 14 minutes or until the cookies are firm to the touch. For even baking, rotate the sheets front to back and top to bottom halfway through. Remove the cookies from the oven and immediately sprinkle each cookie with a pinch of the remaining 1 tablespoon fleur de sel. Allow the cookies to cool slightly on the baking sheets before transferring them to a wire rack to cool completely. The cookies can be stored in an airtight container for up to 2 weeks.

CLASSIC PEANUT BUTTER COOKIES

When you open a bakery there is always the question, "to nut or not to nut?" For us there was only one answer. Allyson is a self-confessed peanut butter junkie, the origins of which can be linked back to a childhood filled with these very cookies. This recipe is a straightforward classic that results in a slightly crisp, slightly soft, golden round of peanut-buttery goodness. A pretty good outcome, addiction notwithstanding.

1 cup all-purpose flour

½ teaspoon baking soda

½ teaspoon salt

½ cup unsalted butter, room temperature

½ cup loosely packed brown sugar

½ cup granulated sugar

1 large egg

1⅓ cups smooth peanut butter

½ teaspoon pure vanilla extract

Tip

This is a great base recipe that lends itself well to experimenting. Go ahead and try crunchy peanut butter in lieu of smooth, or baking in chunks of peanut butter cups.

1. Put oven racks in the middle, upper third and lower third of the oven and preheat the oven to 350°F. Line 2 baking sheets with parchment paper.

2. In a small bowl, whisk together the flour, baking soda and salt.

3. In the bowl of a stand mixer fitted with the paddle attachment, cream the butter, brown sugar and granulated sugar on medium speed until light and fluffy, about 3 minutes. Turn off the mixer and scrape down the sides of the bowl. Add the egg and beat to combine. Add the peanut butter and vanilla and beat to combine. Turn off the mixer and scrape down the sides of the bowl.

4. With the mixer on low speed, slowly add the dry ingredients to the creamed butter mixture, mixing until just combined.

5. Roll the cookie dough into 1-inch balls using your hands or use an ice-cream scoop to portion the dough. Arrange 15 balls on each lined baking sheet, leaving ample space between them. Press down the cookies with a fork in a crosshatch pattern.

6. Bake for 8 to 12 minutes or until the cookies are a light golden brown. For even baking, rotate the sheets front to back and top to bottom halfway through. Allow the cookies to cool slightly on the baking sheets before transferring them to a wire rack to cool completely. The cookies can be stored in an airtight container for up to 5 days.

Photo on page 37.

SOFT & CHEWY
GINGER COOKIES

During the holiday season we can barely keep packages of these ginger cookies on our shelves, and they remain a favourite throughout the year. In fact, one of our parents keeps their bag in the freezer in an attempt to eat only one cookie at a time, a tactic that more often than not fails miserably. What makes this a particularly delicious ginger cookie is the balance of spices and the slightly chewy texture. While ginger is the predominant spice, the addition of cinnamon and cloves results in a more complex and robust flavour, while the molasses adds sweetness and chewy texture.

2¼ cups all-purpose flour

2½ teaspoons baking soda

¾ teaspoon salt

1 tablespoon ground ginger

1½ teaspoons cinnamon

1 teaspoon ground cloves

¾ cup unsalted butter, room temperature

1 cup loosely packed brown sugar

1 large egg

¼ cup fancy molasses

½ cup granulated sugar, for coating cookies

Tip

If you are huge ginger fan, try adding ¼ cup of chopped crystallized ginger with the dry ingredients.

1. In a medium bowl, whisk together the flour, baking soda, salt, ginger, cinnamon and cloves.

2. In the bowl of a stand mixer fitted with the paddle attachment, cream the butter and brown sugar on medium speed until light and fluffy, about 3 minutes. Add the egg and beat to combine. Then add the molasses and mix until incorporated, scraping down the sides of the bowl at least once.

3. With the mixer on low speed, slowly add the dry ingredients to the creamed butter mixture, mixing until just combined. Cover the bowl with plastic wrap and chill in the fridge for 1 hour.

4. Put oven racks in the upper and lower thirds of the oven and preheat the oven to 350°F. Line 2 baking sheets with parchment paper.

5. Roll the dough into 1-inch balls using your hands or use an ice-cream scoop to portion the dough.

6. Place the granulated sugar in a small bowl and roll each ball in the sugar to coat. Arrange 15 balls on each lined baking sheet, leaving ample space between them. If the dough becomes soft or sticky, place it back in the fridge for 15 to 20 minutes to chill before shaping.

7. Bake for 15 to 18 minutes or until the cookies are flattened and doubled in size. For even baking, rotate the sheets front to back and top to bottom halfway through. Allow the cookies to cool slightly on the baking sheets before transferring them to a wire rack to cool completely. The cookies can be stored in an airtight container for up to 2 weeks.

LEMON MADELEINES

This is a simple recipe to make, and we believe our version captures all the best assets of the madeleine. It is light in texture, yet dense enough that it can't be confused with a lemon cake. It is moist and flavourful and has the requisite hump with a slight crack when baked. Madeleines are best enjoyed the day they are baked, but we know that most of you won't eat all of them at one sitting, so we have included a glaze that will prolong their life for a few days.

FOR COATING THE MOULDS

3 tablespoons unsalted butter (approx.), melted

3 tablespoons all-purpose flour (approx.)

MADELEINES

2 cups all-purpose flour

1 teaspoon baking powder

¼ teaspoon salt

1 cup unsalted butter

Zest and juice of 1 lemon

7 large eggs, room temperature

1½ cups granulated sugar

Icing sugar, for dusting (optional)

GLAZE (OPTIONAL)

¾ cup icing sugar

2 tablespoons water

1 tablespoon fresh lemon juice

Tip

Be sure to let the mould chill fully. This not only helps to create the signature hump during baking but also facilitates easy removal of the madeleines.

1. To coat the moulds, lightly brush the indentations of a madeleine mould with some of the melted butter, then lightly dust each indentation with flour. Tap out any access flour. Place the mould in the freezer until you are ready to portion the batter.

2. To make the madeleines, in a medium bowl, whisk together the flour, baking powder and salt.

3. In a small saucepan melt the butter. Remove from the heat and stir in the lemon zest and juice. Leave the mixture to cool.

4. In the bowl of a stand mixer fitted with the whisk attachment, whisk together the eggs and sugar on high speed until the mixture has tripled in volume, 6 to 8 minutes. The mixture should be pale yellow and have reached the ribbon stage (when the whisk is lifted out of the mixture, the batter drops back into the bowl like a falling ribbon).

5. Pour the egg mixture into a wide, shallow bowl. Gently fold in the flour mixture in 3 additions, being careful not to overmix the batter or it will deflate. Drizzle in the lemon/butter mixture in 5 additions, gently folding after each addition to combine. Cover the bowl with plastic wrap and chill for 3 hours.

6. Preheat the oven to 350°F.

7. Spoon batter into each indentation until it's three-quarters full. Do not overfill the indentations or spread the batter (it will spread during baking). If you have 2 moulds, fill them both; they will both fit on the same oven rack. Keep any remaining batter covered in the fridge.

8. Bake, without opening the oven, for 8 to 9 minutes or until the madeleines are lightly golden in colour and the middle has risen in the classic hump. Immediately tap them out of the mould onto a wire rack and allow to cool completely. If you have more batter, wipe out the mould and again coat with butter and flour. Freeze the mould for 30 minutes before filling and baking.

9. Dust the cooled madeleines with icing sugar and serve, or prepare the lemon glaze.

10. To make the glaze, combine the icing sugar, water and lemon juice in a bowl and whisk to combine. Dip the whole cooled madeleines in the glaze. Arrange scallop side up on the wire rack to set. The glazed madeleines can be stored in an airtight container for up to 3 days.

The World's Best

SHORTBREAD COOKIES

We recognize this is a lofty claim, but we remain resolute: this really is the world's best shortbread recipe. One of our Nanas was given this recipe over forty years ago by an elderly friend who, on her deathbed and under cloak of secrecy, was finally willing to part with her much-coveted recipe. We've been thankful ever since. Shortbread is one of the simplest recipes in existence, containing a combination of merely four ingredients—flour, rice flour, butter and sugar. Yet, in what can only be described as pastry alchemy, the perfect ratio of these ingredients and a delicate touch combine to create a light, supremely buttery melt-in-your-mouth shortbread that is beyond compare.

3 cups all-purpose flour

½ cup rice flour

1 pound cold unsalted butter, cut into ½-inch cubes

1¼ cups superfine granulated sugar

Tip

Be sure to use superfine granulated sugar rather than regular granulated sugar. It is much finer and, as such, results in a more delicate texture.

Work the dough as little as possible, and always do so with cold hands.

1. Put oven racks in the upper and lower thirds of the oven and preheat the oven to 300°F. Line 2 baking sheets with parchment paper.

2. In a medium bowl, whisk together the all-purpose flour and rice flour.

3. Place the butter and 1 cup of the sugar in a large bowl and work together with your hands until just combined. Take care not to soften the butter too much with your hands. A delicate touch and cold hands are a must when working with this dough.

4. Using your hands, gradually work the flour mixture into the butter mixture until the dough comes together in a smooth ball.

5. Turn the dough out onto a lightly floured work surface and roll it out to ¼-inch thickness. Using a 2-inch round cookie cutter, cut out 40 rounds. Arrange the cookies on the lined baking sheets, leaving a small space between them. Reroll the scraps and continue to cut out circles until all the dough is used.

6. Bake for 15 to 20 minutes or until the cookies are firm to the touch and they have minimal colouring on them. For even baking, rotate the sheets front to back and top to bottom halfway through. Remove the cookies from the oven and immediately sprinkle with a light coating of the remaining ¼ cup of superfine sugar. Allow the cookies to cool slightly on the baking sheets before transferring them to a wire rack to cool completely. The shortbread can be stored in an airtight container for up to 2 months.

DECORATIVE SUGAR COOKIES

At the shops we make decorative sugar cookies almost every day, whether a monogrammed cookie for a wedding favour or a selection of flower cookies like the ones depicted here. The key to a successful sugar cookie is having a dough that is light and flavourful and that rolls easily, without cracks, but doesn't spread when it's baked. It is imperative that the cookies retain their shape. Those features make this recipe extremely flexible, ensuring that it can be used for a wide variety of projects.

COOKIE DOUGH

3 cups all-purpose flour

1½ teaspoons baking powder

½ teaspoon salt

1 cup unsalted butter, room temperature

1 cup granulated sugar

1 large egg

1 teaspoon pure vanilla extract

ROYAL ICING

Prepare 1 batch (page 238)

Tip

Baked but undecorated sugar cookies can be frozen for up to 3 months.

1. In a medium bowl, whisk together the flour, baking powder and salt.

2. In the bowl of a stand mixer fitted with the paddle attachment, cream the butter and sugar on medium speed until light and fluffy, about 3 minutes. Add the egg and vanilla and beat to combine, stopping once to scrape down the sides of the bowl.

3. With the mixer on low speed, slowly add the flour mixture to the creamed butter mixture, mixing until the dough just comes together. Turn the dough out onto a piece of plastic wrap. Flatten the dough into a disc, wrap fully in the plastic and chill in the fridge for at least 1 hour.

4. Put oven racks in the upper and lower thirds of the oven and preheat the oven to 350°F. Line 2 baking sheets with parchment paper.

5. On a lightly floured work surface, roll out the dough to ¼-inch thickness. (If it starts to crack, let it rest for a few minutes to warm up slightly.) Using a 2-inch round cookie cutter, cut out 36 rounds. Arrange the cookies on the lined baking sheets, leaving a little space between each round.

6. Bake for 15 to 20 minutes or until the cookies are firm to the touch and they have minimal colouring. For even baking, rotate the sheets front to back and top to bottom halfway through. Allow the cookies to cool slightly on the baking sheets before transferring them to a wire rack to cool completely.

7. If you would like to decorate your cookies with a simple royal icing finish; follow the Royal Icing recipe on page 238, including the instructions for turning the royal icing into flood for dipping cookies. If you would like to try the piped flower decoration, turn half the batch of royal icing into flood and follow the steps to the dip the cookies. Use the remaining half to follow the steps on page 219 to create flowers.

PECAN LINZER COOKIES

Often seen at luncheons, showers and holidays, Linzer cookies are the type of delicate cookie you covertly wrap in a napkin and tuck into your purse to enjoy more of later. They are aptly named after the city of Linz in Austria, where they originated as an adaptation of the classic Linzertorte. The cookie always has a nut base, the most popular being almond or hazelnut, but we prefer to use pecans. Toasted pecans enhance the buttery flavour of the cookie and provide a nice contrast to the sweet-tart jam.

1½ cups all-purpose flour

1¼ cups pecans, toasted and finely ground (page 12)

¼ teaspoon cinnamon

¼ teaspoon salt

1 large egg

1 tablespoon cold water

½ cup unsalted butter, room temperature

½ cup granulated sugar

Icing sugar, for dusting

½ cup raspberry jam

Tip

Most Linzers are filled with jams or preserves, but you can also fill them with hazelnut spread or sweetened nut butters.

1. Line 2 baking sheets with parchment paper.

2. In a small bowl, whisk together the flour, pecans, cinnamon and salt. In a small bowl, lightly beat the egg and water with a fork.

3. In the bowl of a stand mixer fitted with the paddle attachment, cream the butter and sugar on medium speed until light and fluffy, about 3 minutes. Add the egg mixture to the creamed butter mixture and beat on medium speed for 1 minute, stopping to scrape down the sides of the bowl at least once.

4. With the mixer on low speed, slowly add the flour mixture to the creamed butter mixture, mixing until just combined and a few dry clumps remain. Do not overwork the dough or it will become tough. Turn the dough out onto a clean, dry work surface and continue bringing it together by hand until it forms a ball. Divide the dough into two balls.

5. Lightly flour your work surface and roll one portion of dough out to ¼-inch thickness. Using a 2-inch fluted round cookie cutter, cut out at least 24 rounds. Then, using the end of a large piping tip or a small fluted cookie cutter, cut out the centres of half the cookies. Transfer all the cookies to the lined baking sheets, leaving a small space between each cookie. Place the cookies in the fridge to chill for at least 20 minutes.

6. Put oven racks in the upper and lower thirds of the oven and preheat the oven to 350°F.

7. Bake the cookies for 11 to 13 minutes or until they are lightly golden and firm to the touch. For even baking, rotate the sheets front to back and top to bottom halfway through. Allow the cookies to cool slightly on the baking sheets before transferring them to a wire rack to cool completely.

8. Repeat steps 5 through 7, using the second portion of dough.

9. Collect the cookies with the hole in the centre and place them right side up on a clean work surface. Using a fine-mesh sieve, lightly dust the tops with icing sugar.

10. Arrange the cookies with no hole in the centre upside down on your work surface. Place the jam in a small bowl and stir with a spoon to loosen it and remove clumps. Stir in a dash of water if the jam is very thick. Place ½ teaspoon of jam in the centre of each cookie. Sandwich with the cookies that have icing sugar on them, being careful not to smudge the sugar. The cookies can be stored in an airtight container for up to 1 week.

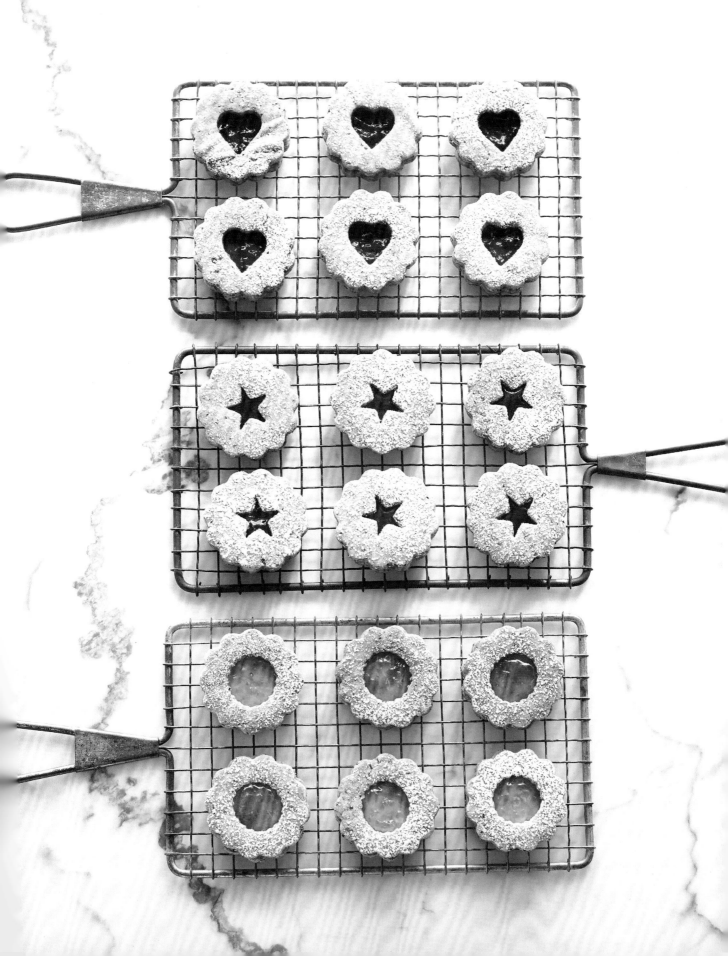

Amaretti cookies are not a home-baked staple in North America, but they have an extensive history in Italy dating back as far as the 1700s. In fact, this humble cookie is the ancestor of the ubiquitous French macaron. Both have an almond base and a slightly chewy texture, but unlike the macaron, amaretti are very simple to make. They pack a ton of flavour thanks to the almond extract and ground almonds, and are the type of cookie you can enjoy daily with tea or coffee much like you would a biscotto. Their pretty white crinkle top also makes them perfect for gifting, or a different addition to a cookie exchange.

AMARETTI

3½ cups ground almonds

1¼ cups granulated sugar

3 large egg whites, room temperature

1 tablespoon almond extract

½ teaspoon pure vanilla extract

SUGAR COATING

3 tablespoons granulated sugar

3 tablespoons icing sugar

Tip

The key to tender, chewy amaretti is not to overwhip the egg whites. They should form stiff peaks but should not be whipped further or they will become dry and separate

1. In a medium bowl, whisk together the ground almonds and sugar.

2. In the bowl of a stand mixer fitted with the whisk attachment, whisk the egg whites until they hold stiff peaks. Transfer the egg whites to a wide, shallow bowl. Gently fold in half of the almond mixture, then fold in the remaining almond mixture. Fold in the almond and vanilla extracts. The dough will be like a thickish paste. Cover the bowl with plastic wrap and chill for 45 minutes.

3. Put oven racks in the upper and lower thirds of the oven and preheat the oven to 350°F. Line 2 baking sheets with parchment paper.

4. Place the granulated sugar and icing sugar on two separate plates. Portion the dough and roll into 1-inch balls or use an ice-cream scoop to portion the dough. Roll each ball in the granulated sugar, then in the icing sugar, and place on a lined baking sheet 3 inches apart. Use the back of a spoon to lightly press down the top of each ball to flatten them ever so slightly.

5. Bake for 15 to 20 minutes or until lightly golden on the edges. For even baking, rotate the sheets front to back and top to bottom hallway through. Allow the cookies to cool slightly on the baking sheets before transferring to a wire rack to cool completely. The cookies can be stored in an airtight container for up to 2 weeks.

Recipe is naturally gluten-free.

Recipe is naturally dairy-free.

HOLIDAY GINGERBREAD HOUSE COOKIES

We all remember making gingerbread houses as kids. It's a common holiday ritual and an opportunity to be creative without pressure. In our homes as kids it was also our moms' secret team-building exercise—sibling group therapy without the pricy bill. Some of that magic has been lost in recent years with the advent of gingerbread-house kits. These prefab creations are indeed a great time saver, but we hope that the tradition of home-baked gingerbread will continue. This dough is easy to make and work with, and it is also delicious. After all, the best part of a homemade gingerbread house is getting to rip it apart and eat it the day after Christmas.

COOKIES

3 cups all-purpose flour

1½ teaspoons baking powder

¾ teaspoon baking soda

½ teaspoon salt

1 tablespoon ground ginger

1 tablespoon cinnamon

¼ teaspoon ground cloves

½ cup unsalted butter, room temperature

¾ cup loosely packed brown sugar

1 large egg, room temperature

½ cup fancy molasses

1 tablespoon pure vanilla extract

ROYAL ICING

Prepare 1 batch (page 238)

Tip

This gingerbread is crisp on the outside and slightly soft on the inside. If you prefer a gingerbread that's crispier throughout, roll the dough slightly thinner. If you're a fan of softer, chewier gingerbread, roll it a bit thicker.

1. In a medium bowl, whisk together the flour, baking powder, baking soda, salt, ginger, cinnamon and cloves until well blended.

2. In the bowl of a stand mixer fitted with the paddle attachment, beat the butter, brown sugar and egg on medium speed until light and fluffy, about 3 minutes. Add the molasses and vanilla and beat until well blended, stopping to scrape down the sides of the bowl midway.

3. With the mixer on low speed, slowly add the flour mixture, mixing until a dough forms. Turn the dough out onto a piece of plastic wrap. Flatten the dough into a disc, fully wrap in the plastic and chill for at least 2 hours or up to 8 hours.

4. Put oven racks in the upper and lower thirds of the oven and preheat the oven to 350°F. Line 2 baking sheets with parchment paper.

5. On a lightly floured work surface, roll out the dough to ¼-inch thickness, using additional flour to dust your work surface and rolling pin as needed. Cut out house shapes, each roughly 3½ × 5 inches, and arrange on the lined baking sheets, leaving a space between each cookie. Gather the scraps, reroll and cut out more houses until all the dough is used. You should have at least 10 cookies.

6. Bake for 15 to 20 minutes or until the cookies are firm to the touch. For even baking, rotate the sheets front to back and top to bottom halfway through. Allow the cookies to cool slightly on the baking sheets before transferring them to a wire rack to cool completely. The cookies can be stored in an airtight container for up to 1 month.

7. To glaze or decorate the cookies with royal icing, follow the instructions on page 238.

Death by Chocolate
BROWNIES

For a long time we didn't sell brownies at Bobbette & Belle because we were never fully satisfied with our test bakes. The brownies were either too dense and fudge-like or too light and cakey. We want to sell only baked goods that we are genuinely excited about, so we left the brownies out until a good client of ours asked us to make them as her wedding favours. Her excitement inspired us to try again, and this time we met with success. Now brownies are a big seller in the shops and in bite-sized versions at events. This recipe is rich and chocolaty, dense but not too dense, and the chocolate ganache glaze takes it over the top. If there's such a thing as death by chocolate, this is how we'd like to go.

BROWNIES

1⅓ cups all-purpose flour

1 cup cocoa powder

¼ teaspoon salt

1 cup unsalted butter, room temperature

3 cups packed brown sugar

1 teaspoon pure vanilla extract

6 large eggs, room temperature

CHOCOLATE GLAZE

Prepare 1 batch (page 239)

Tip

Room-temperature ingredients make for a smoother, creamier batter.

Remember not to overmix the batter once the flour is added or you'll end up with a tough brownie.

1. Preheat the oven to 325°F. Grease a 10-inch square baking pan with butter or non-stick cooking spray and line the bottom with parchment paper.

2. In a small bowl, whisk together the flour, cocoa powder and salt.

3. In the bowl of a stand mixer fitted with the paddle attachment, cream the butter, brown sugar and vanilla on medium speed until light and fluffy, about 3 minutes. Add the eggs one at a time, beating well after each addition. Stop to scrape down the sides of the bowl after the eggs have been added, then beat on medium speed for another 2 minutes.

4. With the mixer on low speed, slowly add the flour mixture to the creamed butter mixture, mixing until just combined. Pour the batter into the prepared pan and spread evenly with a spatula.

5. Bake for 45 minutes or until the brownie is set and a toothpick inserted in the centre comes out with just a few crumbs. Allow the brownie to cool completely in the pan on a wire rack.

6. Once the brownie is cool, turn it out on a wire rack and peel off the parchment paper. Turn the brownie right side up and pour the glaze over the top. Using an offset spatula, smooth the glaze evenly to the edges. Place the brownie in the fridge for 20 minutes to fully set the glaze before cutting into squares. The glazed brownies can be stored in a single layer in an airtight container for up to 1 week.

PECAN CARAMEL
CHURCHILL SQUARES

Most sweet lovers have had a pecan caramel square at one point or another. The ingredients and method don't vary much from recipe to recipe, so it came as a huge surprise several years ago when we tasted the best pecan caramel square ever. It consisted of a buttery shortbread base, chewy caramel, toasted pecans and just the right amount of dark chocolate drizzled on top. Mrs. Churchill is a wedding industry peer of ours, and every year she would save us samples of her delicious pecan squares to nibble on during long wedding shows. We made it a goal to include in this book a pecan square recipe that would do her proud. We think we hit the nail on the head. Let us know, Mrs. Churchill!

SHORTBREAD CRUST

2¼ cups all-purpose flour

½ cup granulated sugar

¾ teaspoon salt

¾ cup cold unsalted butter, cut into
1-inch cubes

2 to 4 tablespoons ice water

PECAN CARAMEL TOPPING

1¼ cups loosely packed brown sugar

¾ cup unsalted butter

½ cup honey

½ teaspoon salt

1 cup 35% cream

2¼ cups chopped pecans

CHOCOLATE GARNISH

¼ cup chopped dark chocolate (2 ounces)

Tip

These squares have a great shelf life and transport well. They make particularly nice gifts for someone lucky, or include them in a baking exchange.

1. Preheat the oven to 325°F. Grease a 10-inch square baking pan with butter or non-stick cooking spray and line the bottom with parchment paper.

2. To make the crust, in a medium bowl whisk together the flour, sugar and salt until well blended. Add the cold butter and blend into the flour with your hands until the mixture resembles coarse meal. Sprinkle with 2 tablespoons of the cold water and gently knead until the dough just comes together and there are no dry clumps, sprinkling in more water as necessary. Do not let the dough become overly sticky. Press the dough evenly into the bottom of the prepared pan.

3. Bake for 25 minutes or until the crust is a light golden colour. For even baking, rotate the pan front to back halfway through. Allow to cool completely in the pan on a wire rack. (Do not turn off the oven.)

4. To make the pecan caramel topping, in a small saucepan combine the brown sugar, butter, honey and salt. Bring to a boil over medium-high heat, stirring constantly, and cook until foamy and slightly thickened, about 10 minutes. Slowly pour in the cream and continue to cook, stirring occasionally, for 10 minutes, until a candy thermometer reads 240°F. Add the pecans and cook for 2 minutes longer, stirring constantly. Pour the topping over the cooled crust, spreading it evenly with a spatula.

5. Bake for 10 minutes or until the topping is bubbling. Allow to cool completely in the pan on a wire rack.

6. To make the chocolate garnish, melt the chocolate in a microwave oven or in a double boiler.

7. Turn the cooled square out on a wire rack and peel off the parchment paper, then turn it right side up on a cutting board. Drizzle with the chocolate and allow it to set for several minutes. Cut into squares. The squares can be stored in an airtight container for up to 2 weeks.

DATE SQUARES

All hail the humble date square! This familiar yet often overlooked square may be the unfortunate slightly homely sibling of more decadent squares, yet it provides the cornerstone of coffeehouse sweets across North America. There's a reason for this: it's delicious! It also has the benefit of being vaguely healthy. All those dates and oats must be good for you, right? Calories notwithstanding, the date square is a sweet that you can enjoy any time of day. It's sweet, but not cloyingly so, and it has a wonderful crunchy yet soft texture that leaves your sweet tooth satisfied without all the usual guilt.

DATE FILLING

2½ cups pitted dates

1 cup water

2 tablespoons brown sugar

2 tablespoons fresh lemon juice

½ teaspoon baking soda

OAT CRUMBLE TOPPING

1¾ cups large-flake rolled oats

1 cup all-purpose flour

¾ cup loosely packed brown sugar

¼ teaspoon baking powder

¾ cup unsalted butter, cut into chunks, room temperature

Tip

Try switching out the dates for an equal amount of prunes.

1. Preheat the oven to 350°F. Grease an 8-inch square baking pan with butter or non-stick cooking spray and line the bottom with parchment paper.

2. To make the filling, combine the dates, water, brown sugar and lemon juice in a saucepan and bring to a boil. Reduce the heat to medium and stir in the baking soda. Continue to cook, stirring occasionally, until the dates are soft and start to lose their shape, about 5 minutes. Remove from the heat and allow the filling to cool completely.

3. To make the crumble topping, whisk together the oats, flour, brown sugar and baking powder until combined. Add the butter and mix in with your hands until it forms a crumble.

4. Divide the crumble in half and firmly press one half evenly into the bottom of the baking pan. Evenly spread the cooled date mixture over the base, and then sprinkle with the remaining crumble topping, pressing lightly.

5. Bake for 50 to 60 minutes or until the topping is a light golden colour. For even baking, rotate the pan front to back halfway through. Allow to cool completely in the pan on a wire rack before removing from the pan and cutting into squares. The squares can be stored in an airtight container for up to 2 weeks.

CINNAMON PINWHEELS

Reduce, reuse, recycle—that is the mantra of our generation. Having grown up in a consumerist culture, we often have to consciously think about not being wasteful, but many of our grandmas, who lived through the Great Depression, found ingenious ways to use up even the smallest of leftovers. As a child, Allyson would sometimes come home from school to find her Nana working intently, huddled over pies ... lots and lots of pies. The mere sight evoked only one response, usually screeched loudly with limbs flailing: "Nana, make WHEELS!" Nana's leftover pastry dough always became Cinnamon Pinwheels, an intoxicating combination of flaky dough, butter, sugar and cinnamon—the cookie equivalent of a cinnamon bun. They're so good, we felt they finally deserved to be a recipe in their own right. No pies required.

2½ cups all-purpose flour

2 teaspoons granulated sugar

¾ teaspoon salt

1 cup cold unsalted butter, cut into 1-inch cubes

⅓ cup + 1 tablespoon ice water

2 tablespoons unsalted butter (approx.), melted

¾ cup loosely packed brown sugar

4½ teaspoons cinnamon

Tip

The rolled-up sausage can be refrigerated for up to 3 days or frozen for up to 1 month. Let it sit, wrapped and at room temperature, until it is easy to cut through.

1. In a medium bowl, whisk together the flour, granulated sugar and salt. Add the butter and blend with a pastry cutter until the mixture forms pea-sized clumps. Add the water a little at a time and mix in with your hands until the dough just starts to stick together. The key to a great pinwheel is being gentle with the dough and not overworking it. Add 1 to 2 tablespoons more ice water if the dough seems dry and won't come together.

2. Turn the dough out onto a work surface and push it together with your hands until it forms a ball. Do not knead the dough—simply push it together. Flatten the dough into a disc, wrap in plastic wrap and chill for at least 1 hour.

3. On a lightly floured work surface, roll the dough into a 15- × 20-inch rectangle that is ¼-inch thick. Brush the melted butter all over the dough, going right to the edges.

4. In a small bowl, blend together the brown sugar and cinnamon. Sprinkle the cinnamon sugar evenly over the dough, going right to the edges. Starting on a long side, roll up the dough in a tight sausage, pressing the seam to seal. Wrap in plastic wrap and chill in the freezer for 30 minutes.

5. Put oven racks in the upper and lower thirds of the oven and preheat the oven to 375°F. Line 2 baking sheets with parchment paper.

6. Remove the plastic wrap and cut the sausage crosswise into ½-inch slices. Arrange the pinwheels 3 inches apart on the lined baking sheets.

7. Bake for 18 to 22 minutes or until lightly golden brown. For even baking, rotate the sheets front to back and top to bottom halfway through. Allow the pinwheels to cool slightly on the baking sheets before transferring them to a wire rack to cool completely. The pinwheels can be stored in an airtight container for up to 2 weeks.

2

CUPCAKES

VANILLA BIRTHDAY CUPCAKES

We are both, without a doubt, chocolate people. However, when it came time to developing a birthday cupcake, we both agreed that it had to be a light, fluffy vanilla cake with vanilla frosting and rainbow sprinkles. Something about that combination is so evocative of childhood, when you would count down the days until your birthday and couldn't wait to blow out the candles. Nowadays the sheer number of candles for us would be a fire hazard, but we still relish this tasty little cupcake, knowing, just as we did as kids, that sprinkles make everything better.

CUPCAKES

1 cup + 2 tablespoons all-purpose flour

1¼ teaspoons baking powder

¼ teaspoon salt

1 large egg, room temperature

1 tablespoon lightly beaten egg white, room temperature

½ cup unsalted butter, room temperature

¾ cup granulated sugar

1 teaspoon pure vanilla extract

⅔ cup whole milk, room temperature

2 tablespoons rainbow sprinkles, for garnish

CLASSIC VANILLA FROSTING

Prepare 1 batch (page 229)

Tip

If you want a really fun birthday surprise, stir coloured sprinkles right into the cupcake batter. Approximately ⅓ cup should do the trick.

1. Preheat the oven to 350°F. Line a cupcake pan with 12 cupcake liners.

2. In a medium bowl, whisk together the flour, baking powder and salt. In a small bowl, lightly beat together the egg and egg white.

3. In the bowl of a stand mixer fitted with the paddle attachment, cream the butter and sugar on medium speed until light and fluffy, about 3 minutes. Beat in the eggs in 3 additions, stopping after each addition to scrape down the sides of the bowl. Add the vanilla and beat until well combined.

4. With the mixer on low speed, alternate adding the flour mixture in 3 additions and the milk in 2 additions, beginning and ending with the flour mixture. Blend after each addition until just combined, stopping the mixer to scrape down the sides of the bowl at least once. Using a spoon, divide batter evenly between the cupcake liners, filling approximately three-quarters full.

5. Bake for 20 minutes or until a toothpick inserted in the centre comes out clean. For even baking, rotate the pan front to back halfway through. Allow the cupcakes to cool in the pan for 10 minutes before turning them out onto a wire rack to cool completely.

6. Frost the cooled cupcakes using a spoon, a small offset spatula or a piping bag and tip. Apply the sprinkles to each cupcake as it's frosted. The cupcakes can be stored in an airtight container for up to 3 days.

PIPED ROSE LEMON CUPCAKES

Often when a bride is looking for a cupcake tower for her wedding, we recommend using a mix of mini and regular-size cupcakes. Minis are easier for guests to navigate and there is less chance of accidental stains. These lemon cupcakes are the perfect little two-bite treat, and they look as though they were plucked fresh from the garden. At Bobbette & Belle we are known for our highly decorative desserts, so no book would seem complete without a few decorative desserts.

CUPCAKES

1 cup all-purpose flour

½ teaspoon baking soda

⅓ cup unsalted butter, room temperature

1 cup granulated sugar (reserve ¼ cup)

3 large eggs, separated, room temperature

⅓ cup sour cream

1½ teaspoons lemon zest

2 tablespoons fresh lemon juice

1½ teaspoons pure vanilla extract

LEMON BUTTERCREAM

Prepare 1 batch of Classic Vanilla Buttercream (page 222)

½ cup fresh lemon juice

Food colouring in the amount and colour of your choice.

Tip

The nice thing about lemon cupcakes is that they pack a lot of flavour but are neutral in colour. By adding some food colouring to the lemon buttercream, you can create whatever colour palate you like.

1. Preheat the oven to 350°F. Line a mini cupcake pan with 24 mini cupcake liners.

2. In a small bowl, whisk together the flour and baking soda.

3. In the bowl of a stand mixer fitted with the paddle attachment, cream the butter and ¾ cup of the sugar on medium speed until light and fluffy, about 3 minutes. Add the egg yolks one at a time, beating well after each addition. Scrape down the sides of the bowl. Add the sour cream, lemon zest, lemon juice and vanilla and beat until combined.

4. With the mixer on low speed, add the flour mixture in 3 additions, beating after each addition until combined. Stop to scrape down the sides of the bowl as needed. Scrape the batter into a large bowl and set aside.

5. Thoroughly clean and dry the mixer bowl. Using the whisk attachment, whisk the egg whites on medium-high speed until soft peaks form, about 2 minutes. Add the reserved ¼ cup of sugar in a slow, thin, even stream. Continue to whisk on medium-high speed until the meringue is glossy and holds stiff peaks.

6. Gently fold a bit of the meringue into the batter to lighten it. Gently but thoroughly fold in the remaining meringue, being careful to not overmix the batter or it will deflate. Using a teaspoon, divide batter evenly between the cupcake liners, filling approximately three-quarters full. (For more control, place some of the batter in a resealable plastic bag and cut a dime-sized hole in one corner to allow the batter to be piped cleanly into the small liners.)

7. Bake for 20 minutes or until a toothpick inserted in the centre comes out clean. For even baking, rotate the pan front to back halfway through. Allow the cupcakes to cool in the pan for 10 minutes before turning them out onto a wire rack to cool completely.

8. Whisk the lemon juice into the buttercream by hand, then tint the buttercream using one or more food colourings. (For the photo, we used red and yellow to create three shades of pink, peach and coral.) Ice the cooled cupcakes using a spoon, a small offset spatula or a piping bag and tip. If you would like to decorate the cupcakes with the rose technique depicted, follow the instructions on page 219. The cupcakes can be stored in an airtight container in the fridge for up to 3 days.

DOUBLE CHOCOLATE CUPCAKES

When Sarah was a child, one of her favourite treats was a Dairy Queen dipped cone. To this day, even with a production kitchen full of the world's best coverture, when we're out on delivery she will still shout with glee, "Oooh look, Dairy Queen!" if she happens to see one. There is no judgment here, given that we both had what we aptly describe as church-basement childhoods filled with Company's Coming squares and Sex in a Pan. Our goal is not to deny these humble culinary beginnings, but instead to elevate. This cupcake is all the best parts of a dipped cone, only elevated with moist chocolate cake, creamy whipped chocolate buttercream and yummy chocolate ganache coating.

CUPCAKES

1 cup all-purpose flour

1 cup granulated sugar

3 tablespoons cocoa powder

1 teaspoon baking soda

½ teaspoon baking powder

½ teaspoon salt

1 large egg, room temperature

½ cup buttermilk, room temperature

½ cup hot brewed coffee (instant or drip)

¼ cup vegetable oil

½ teaspoon pure vanilla extract

CHOCOLATE BUTTERCREAM

Prepare 1 batch (page 223)

CHOCOLATE GLAZE

Prepare 1 batch (page 239)

Tip

You could use store-bought chocolate crackle topping, but resist. The homemade chocolate glaze is truly worth the effort, as it really enhances the rich, dark chocolate flavour of this cupcake.

1. Preheat the oven to 350°F. Line a cupcake pan with 12 cupcake liners.

2. Before you place the bowl of a stand mixer on the stand, combine in the bowl the flour, sugar, cocoa powder, baking soda, baking powder and salt and whisk together. In a separate bowl, whisk together the egg, buttermilk, hot coffee, vegetable oil and vanilla. Add the wet mixture to the dry mixture and whisk to incorporate the ingredients.

3. Fit the mixer with the paddle attachment, then beat the batter on medium-low speed for 2 minutes, until it is well combined and smooth. Do not overmix the batter by beating on high speed. Using a spoon, divide batter evenly between the cupcake liners, filling approximately three-quarters full.

4. Bake for 20 minutes or until a toothpick inserted in the centre comes out clean. For even baking, rotate the pan front to back halfway through. Allow the cupcakes to cool in the pan for 10 minutes before turning them out onto a wire rack to cool completely.

5. Ice the cooled cupcakes with the chocolate buttercream using a spoon, a small offset spatula or a piping bag and tip. Place the iced cupcakes in the fridge to chill for 20 minutes. (This will make the buttercream stable for dipping in the glaze.)

6. Working quickly so the buttercream stays chilled, invert the chilled cupcakes one at a time and dip the entire buttercream top in and out of the chocolate glaze in one steady motion. Hold the inverted cupcake over the bowl until it stops dripping, then turn it right side up and set it aside on a tray. Continue until all the cupcakes are dipped. Return the dipped cupcakes to the fridge and chill for another 10 minutes or until the glaze is fully set. Bring the cupcakes to room temperature before serving. The cupcakes can be stored in an airtight container in the fridge for up to 3 days.

CAFFÈ LATTE CUPCAKES

In North America coffee reigns supreme as the drink of choice for many people. Drip coffee from the pot with breakfast, latte at lunch, a mid-afternoon macchiato pick-me-up. But for all that love of coffee, very few desserts feature it as the star. This is unfortunate, given that coffee, much like pure cocoa, is a distinctive strong and bitter flavour that is greatly enhanced when paired with sugars and fats. Also like chocolate, the flavour is affected by roasting and origin, which allow for a multitude of flavour variations. We wanted to create a cupcake that would both feature and enhance the coffee flavour. The brown sugar in both the cupcake and the buttercream brings out the caramel notes in the coffee and gives it a softer flavour, much the way a latte does.

CUPCAKES

1½ cups all-purpose flour

1½ teaspoons baking soda

¼ teaspoon salt

1¼ cups loosely packed brown sugar

2 large egg whites, room temperature

¾ cup buttermilk, room temperature

1 tablespoon pure vanilla extract

½ cup unsalted butter, melted and cooled

ESPRESSO AND BROWN SUGAR BUTTERCREAM

Prepare 1 batch Brown Sugar Buttercream (page 226), adding 1 tablespoon coffee extract along with the vanilla (see source guide, page 248)

Tip

You can use instant espresso powder or even instant coffee to flavour the buttercream, but if you're a coffee connoisseur we recommend sourcing a high-quality coffee extract such as the one made by Nielsen-Massey.

1. Preheat the oven to 350°F. Line a cupcake pan with 12 cupcake liners.

2. In a small bowl, whisk together the flour, baking soda and salt.

3. In a large bowl, whisk together the brown sugar and egg whites until smooth. Add the buttermilk and vanilla and whisk until fully combined. Add the melted butter and whisk until fully incorporated. Add the flour mixture in 3 additions, mixing together and scraping the sides of the bowl as necessary. Using a spoon, divide batter evenly between the cupcake liners, filling approximately three-quarters full.

4. Bake for 20 minutes or until a toothpick inserted in the centre comes out clean. For even baking, rotate the pan front to back halfway through. Allow the cupcakes to cool in the pan for 10 minutes before turning them out onto a wire rack to cool completely.

5. Ice the cooled cupcakes using a spoon, a small offset spatula or a piping bag and tip. The cupcakes can be stored in an airtight container in the fridge for up to 3 days.

PEANUT BUTTER CHOCOLATE CUPCAKES

Chocolate and peanut butter may seem a little pedestrian at times, but all it takes is a quick Internet search and you'll find thousands of recipes devoted to this pairing. In fact, there are so many over-the-top combinations that it is easy to lose sight of how wonderful this marriage is in its simplest form. This chocolate cupcake with peanut butter frosting highlights the best part of each component—the slight bitterness of the chocolate and the creamy sweetness of the peanut butter. It is the type of cupcake that is impossible to eat just one of.

CUPCAKES

1 cup all-purpose flour

1 cup granulated sugar

3 tablespoons cocoa powder

1 teaspoon baking soda

½ teaspoon baking powder

½ teaspoon salt

1 large egg, room temperature

½ cup buttermilk, room temperature

½ cup hot brewed coffee (instant or drip)

¼ cup vegetable oil

½ teaspoon pure vanilla extract

PEANUT BUTTER FROSTING

Prepare 1 batch (page 233)

Tip

To take the peanut butter factor to the next level, garnish with mini peanut butter cups, or hide one in the centre of each cupcake before baking.

1. Preheat the oven to 350°F. Line a cupcake pan with 12 cupcake liners.

2. Before you place the bowl of a stand mixer on the stand, combine in the bowl the flour, sugar, cocoa powder, baking soda, baking powder and salt and whisk together. In a separate bowl, whisk together the egg, buttermilk, hot coffee, vegetable oil and vanilla. Add the wet mixture to the dry mixture and whisk to incorporate the ingredients.

3. Fit the mixer with the paddle attachment, then beat the batter on medium-low speed for 2 minutes, until it is well combined and smooth. Do not overmix the batter by beating on high speed. Using a spoon, divide batter evenly between the cupcake liners, filling approximately three-quarters full.

4. Bake for 20 minutes or until a toothpick inserted in the centre comes out clean. For even baking, rotate the pan front to back halfway through. Allow the cupcakes to cool in the pan for 10 minutes before turning them out onto a wire rack to cool completely.

5. Frost the cooled cupcakes using a spoon, a small offset spatula or a piping bag and tip. The cupcakes can be stored in an airtight container in the fridge for up to 3 days.

MINT CHOCOLATE CUPCAKES

Sarah is a mint chocolate fanatic, which is evidenced by the half-eaten bag of York Peppermint Patties often to be found beside her. She is also a true sugar addict, not in the occupational-hazard way of a pastry chef but more like in an alcoholic-working-at-a-bar kind of way. Needless to say, she took the lead on this recipe, tweaking the ratio of mint to sugar to chocolate until it met her exacting standards. We have called these "holiday" cupcakes because they would be the perfect treat for anyone that time of year. But for mint lovers like Sarah, they are the perfect treat any time of the year.

CUPCAKES

1 cup all-purpose flour

1 cup granulated sugar

3 tablespoons cocoa powder

1 teaspoon baking soda

½ teaspoon baking powder

½ teaspoon salt

1 large egg, room temperature

½ cup buttermilk, room temperature

½ cup hot brewed coffee (instant or drip)

¼ cup vegetable oil

½ teaspoon pure vanilla extract

MINT FROSTING

Prepare 1 batch (page 234)

Mint chocolate cupcakes are great any time of year, but garnishing them with candy cane pieces at Christmas makes them especially festive.

Add ¼ cup mint-flavoured chocolate chips to the batter for even more mint flavour.

1. Preheat the oven to 350°F. Line a cupcake pan with 12 cupcake liners.

2. Before you place the bowl of a stand mixer on the stand, combine in the bowl the flour, sugar, cocoa powder, baking soda, baking powder and salt and whisk together. In a separate bowl, whisk together the egg, buttermilk, hot coffee, vegetable oil and vanilla. Add the wet mixture to the dry mixture and whisk to incorporate the ingredients.

3. Fit the mixer with the paddle attachment, then beat the batter on medium-low speed for 2 minutes, until it is well combined and smooth. Do not overmix the batter by beating on high speed. Using a spoon, divide batter evenly between the cupcake liners, filling approximately three-quarters full.

4. Bake for 20 minutes or until a toothpick inserted in the centre comes out clean. For even baking, rotate the pan front to back halfway through. Allow the cupcakes to cool in the pan for 10 minutes before turning them out onto a wire rack to cool completely.

5. Frost the cooled cupcakes using a spoon, a small offset spatula or a piping bag and tip. The cupcakes can be stored in an airtight container in the fridge for up to 3 days.

SALTED CARAMEL CUPCAKES

We often say that, as business partners, we are two halves of the same whole and, at the risk of sounding as sappy as Tom Cruise did, we complete each other, at least as far as our palates go. Thankfully we enjoy a lot of the same flavours, but we also each have a list of things that we particularly like as individuals. For Allyson, one of those things is definitely salted caramel. If you look at our recipes or come into the shops you will notice a variety of items with caramel and fleur de sel, whether used as a garnish or as a component in a recipe. The nice thing about this salted caramel cupcake is that it puts the caramel at the forefront and highlights how wonderful a homemade version is.

CUPCAKES

1 cup + 2 tablespoons all-purpose flour

1¼ teaspoons baking powder

¼ teaspoon salt

1 large egg, room temperature

1 tablespoon lightly beaten egg white, room temperature

½ cup unsalted butter, room temperature

¾ cup granulated sugar

1 teaspoon pure vanilla extract

⅔ cup whole milk, room temperature

3 tablespoons toffee pieces

SALTED CARAMEL BUTTERCREAM

Prepare 1 batch (page 225)

SALTED CARAMEL SAUCE

Prepare ½ batch (page 190) or use store-bought caramel and add salt to taste

1. Preheat the oven to 350°F. Line a cupcake pan with 12 cupcake liners.

2. In a medium bowl, whisk together the flour, baking powder and salt. In a small bowl, lightly beat together the egg and egg white.

3. In the bowl of a stand mixer fitted with the paddle attachment, cream the butter and sugar on medium speed until light and fluffy, about 3 minutes. Beat in the eggs in 3 additions, stopping after each addition to scrape down the sides of the bowl. Add the vanilla and beat until well combined.

4. With the mixer on low speed, alternate adding the flour mixture in 3 additions and the milk in 2 additions, beginning and ending with the flour mixture. Blend after each addition until just combined, stopping the mixer to scrape down the sides of the bowl at least once. Add the toffee pieces and mix for 15 seconds to combine. Using a spoon, divide batter evenly between the cupcake liners, filling approximately three-quarters full.

5. Bake for 20 minutes or until a toothpick inserted in the centre comes out clean. For even baking, rotate the pan front to back halfway through. Allow the cupcakes to cool in the pan for 10 minutes before turning them out onto a rack to cool completely.

6. Ice the cooled cupcakes using a spoon, a small offset spatula or a piping bag and tip. Drizzle the cupcakes with the salted caramel sauce. The cupcakes can be stored in an airtight container in the fridge for up to 3 days.

Tip   The homemade salted caramel sauce can also be used as a filling if you want a real burst of caramel flavour. Simply use a sharp paring knife to cut out a dime-size tunnel in the centre of each cooled cupcake, going about halfway down. Using a piping bag, fill the hole with caramel sauce, then ice on top with the salted caramel buttercream.

PINK CHAMPAGNE CUPCAKES

Our dear friend Erica, with a measure of awe, refers to impressively stylish women in her social circle as "fancy ladies." We love the idea of a "fancy ladies" cupcake, a recipe that is simple enough to please a lot of palates but distinctive and pretty enough to be served at special events like showers and luncheons. Enter the Pink Champagne Cupcake: light pink chiffon cake topped with pink champagne frosting. A dessert worthy of Erica, who, truth be told, is the fanciest lady we know.

CUPCAKES

1¼ cups all-purpose flour

1½ teaspoons baking powder

¼ teaspoon salt

⅔ cup whole milk, room temperature

1 teaspoon pure vanilla extract

2 drops red food colouring

½ cup unsalted butter, room temperature

1 cup granulated sugar (reserve ¼ cup)

3 large egg whites, room temperature

PINK CHAMPAGNE FROSTING

Prepare 1 batch (page 230)

Tip

For a pretty garnish, separate the petals from a pesticide-free rose or other edible flower, brush them with a thin layer of egg white and dip in granulated sugar. Set them aside to dry for 30 minutes.

1. Preheat the oven to 350°F. Line a cupcake pan with 12 cupcake liners.

2. In a small bowl, whisk together the flour, baking powder and salt. In a measuring cup, stir together the milk, vanilla and food colouring.

3. In the bowl of a stand mixer fitted with the paddle attachment, cream the butter and ¾ cup of the sugar on medium speed until light and fluffy, about 3 minutes.

4. With the mixer on low speed, alternate adding the flour mixture in 3 additions and the milk mixture in 2 additions, beginning and ending with the flour mixture. Blend after each addition until just combined, stopping the mixer to scrape down the sides of the bowl at least once. Scrape the batter into a large bowl and set aside.

5. Thoroughly clean and dry the mixer bowl. Using the whisk attachment, whisk the egg whites on medium-high speed until soft peaks form, about 2 minutes. Add the reserved ¼ cup of sugar in a slow, thin, even stream. Continue to whisk on medium-high speed until the meringue is glossy and holds stiff peaks.

6. Gently fold a bit of the meringue into the batter to lighten it. Gently but thoroughly fold in the remaining meringue, being careful to not overmix the batter or it will deflate. Using a spoon, divide batter evenly between the cupcake liners, filling approximately three-quarters full.

7. Bake for 20 minutes or until a toothpick inserted in the centre comes out clean. For even baking, rotate the pan front to back halfway through. Allow the cupcakes to cool in the pan for 10 minutes before turning them out onto a wire rack to cool completely.

8. Frost the cooled cupcakes using a spoon, a small offset spatula or a piping bag and tip. The cupcakes can be stored in an airtight container in the fridge for up to 3 days.

SUNDAE CUPCAKES

A sundae is an edible canvas that's a vessel for a wide variety of yummy fillings and toppings to shine. In that vein, our cupcake version is classic vanilla, but that is where the ordinary ends. We fill our cupcake with strawberry jam and top it with chocolate glaze and sprinkles. But the really fun thing about this recipe is that it allows you to be creative.

CUPCAKES

1 cup + 2 tablespoons all-purpose flour

1¼ teaspoons baking powder

¼ teaspoon salt

1 large egg, room temperature

1 tablespoon lightly beaten egg white, room temperature

½ cup unsalted butter, room temperature

¾ cup granulated sugar

1 teaspoon pure vanilla extract

⅔ cup whole milk, room temperature

STRAWBERRY FILLING

¾ cup strawberry jam

CLASSIC VANILLA BUTTERCREAM

Prepare 1 batch (page 222)

CHOCOLATE GLAZE

Prepare ½ batch (page 239)

GARNISH

¼ cup rainbow sprinkles

12 whole fresh cherries with stems

1. Preheat the oven to 350°F. Line a cupcake pan with 12 cupcake liners.

2. In a medium bowl, whisk together the flour, baking powder and salt. In a small bowl, lightly beat together the eggs and egg white.

3. In the bowl of a stand mixer fitted with the paddle attachment, cream the butter and sugar on medium speed until light and fluffy, about 3 minutes. Beat in the eggs in 3 additions, stopping after each addition to scrape down the sides of the bowl. Add the vanilla and beat until well combined.

4. With the mixer on low speed, alternate adding the flour mixture in 3 additions and the milk in 2 additions, beginning and ending with the flour mixture. Blend after each addition until just combined, stopping the mixer to scrape down the sides of the bowl at least once. Using a spoon, divide the batter evenly between the cupcake liners, filling approximately three-quarters full.

5. Bake for 20 minutes or until a toothpick inserted in the centre comes out clean. For even baking, rotate the pan front to back halfway through. Allow the cupcakes to cool in the pan for 10 minutes before turning them out onto a wire rack to cool completely.

6. To fill the cooled cupcakes with the strawberry jam, use a small paring knife to cut out a small tunnel in the centre of each cupcake, going about halfway down. Spoon 1 tablespoon of jam into each cupcake.

7. Frost the cupcakes with the buttercream using a spoon, a small offset spatula or a piping bag and tip.

8. Using a spoon, top the frosted cupcakes with the chocolate glaze, allowing it to run down over the buttercream. Garnish the cupcakes with sprinkles and a cherry, or other garnishes of your choice. The cupcakes can be stored in an airtight container in the fridge for up to 3 days.

Tip For the photo, we placed our baked cupcakes in glass sundae dishes, but you could also bake them in small oven-safe white ramekins. Or turn them into ice-cream cones by baking them in classic flat-bottom ice-cream cones. Simply place the cones in muffin cups and surround with a little tin foil for stability. Bake as usual.

SOUTHERN RED VELVET CUPCAKES

Red velvet cake is traditionally thought of as a southern cake, although the Waldorf Astoria Hotel in New York is actually credited with its invention. The red colour is thought to have been derived from the red tint of the cocoa used in early recipes, which is activated by the vinegar. Over the years the red colour has become more pronounced and the cream cheese topping has become an integral part of the recipe. When we started making red velvet we thought it might be a short-lived trend, but now we recognize it owes its longevity to the fact that it appeals to so many palates. It is a supremely moist cake that is a perfect balance between vanilla and chocolate.

CUPCAKES

1 cup all-purpose flour

4½ teaspoons cocoa powder

1 teaspoon baking soda

¼ teaspoon salt

½ cup buttermilk, room temperature

1 teaspoon red food colouring

1 teaspoon white vinegar

1 teaspoon pure vanilla extract

⅓ cup vegetable oil

¾ cup granulated sugar

2 large eggs, room temperature

COOKED CREAM CHEESE FROSTING

Prepare 1 batch (page 236)

Tip

If you prefer, swap out the cooked frosting for the Cream Cheese Buttercream on page 227.

1. Preheat the oven to 350°F. Line a cupcake pan with 12 cupcake liners.

2. In a small bowl, whisk together the flour, cocoa powder, baking soda and salt. In a measuring cup, combine the buttermilk, food colouring, vinegar and vanilla.

3. In the bowl of a stand mixer fitted with the paddle attachment, mix the vegetable oil and sugar on medium speed until well combined. Add the eggs one at a time, mixing well after each addition.

4. With the mixer on low speed, alternate adding the flour mixture in 3 additions and the milk mixture in 2 additions, beginning and ending with the flour mixture. Blend after each addition until just combined, stopping the mixer to scrape down the sides of the bowl at least once. Do not overmix the batter. Using a spoon, divide the batter evenly between the cupcake liners, filling approximately two-thirds full.

5. Bake for 20 minutes or until a toothpick inserted in the centre comes out clean. For even baking, rotate the pan front to back halfway through. Allow the cupcakes to cool in the pan for 10 minutes before turning them out onto a wire rack to cool completely.

6. Ice the cooled cupcakes using a spoon, a small offset spatula or a piping bag and tip. Because of the cream cheese in the buttercream, the iced cupcakes may be kept at room temperature for up to 3 hours; after that, they should be stored in an airtight container in the fridge. Bring the cupcakes to room temperature before serving. The cupcakes can be stored in an airtight container in the fridge for up to 3 days.

CLASSIC HUMMINGBIRD CUPCAKES

We have both long had a passion for baking history and researching the origins of particular desserts. For several years we have been talking about hummingbird cake. It is thought of as a traditional southern cake, but its origins can be traced to Jamaica, where its two key ingredients, bananas and pineapple, are plentiful. Neither of us had ever encountered one in Canada, nor had we tried it ourselves, but we felt certain that the ingredients were a winning combination. So we set out to develop a recipe that would be easy to make and would act as a nice alternative to carrot cake. What takes our version several notches up are the coconut, which helps to balance out the banana flavour, and the addictive sour cream frosting, our twist on the traditional cream cheese frosting.

CUPCAKES

1 cup all-purpose flour

¾ teaspoon baking soda

½ teaspoon salt

¼ teaspoon cinnamon

⅔ cup granulated sugar

1 large egg, room temperature

⅓ cup vegetable oil

1 teaspoon pure vanilla extract

⅔ cup canned crushed pineapple (not drained)

⅓ cup mashed ripe banana

⅓ cup finely chopped pecans

⅓ cup flaked coconut

SOUR CREAM FROSTING

Make 1 batch (page 235)

Tip

This is a quick and easy batter that can be mixed by hand if you do not have a stand mixer. It also bakes up wonderfully as a single layer cake in a square pan.

1. Preheat the oven to 350°F. Line a cupcake pan with 12 cupcake liners.

2. In a bowl, whisk together the flour, baking soda, salt and cinnamon.

3. In the bowl of a stand mixer fitted with the paddle attachment, combine the sugar, egg, vegetable oil and vanilla. Beat on medium-low speed until creamy. Turn the mixer to low speed and add the flour mixture in thirds, mixing after each addition until just combined. Add the crushed pineapple, mashed banana, pecans and coconut. Mix until just combined. Using a spoon, divide the batter evenly between the cupcake liners, filling approximately three-quarters full.

4. Bake for 18 to 20 minutes or until lightly golden and a toothpick inserted in the centre comes out clean. For even baking, rotate the pan front to back halfway through. Allow the cupcakes to cool in the pan for 10 minutes before turning them out onto a wire rack to cool completely.

5. Frost the cooled cupcakes using a spoon, a small offset spatula or a piping bag and tip. The cupcakes can be stored in an airtight container in the fridge for up to 3 days.

3

LAYER CAKES

Classic Vanilla
Layer Cake
• 82 •

Caramel
Apple Cake
• 92 •

Dark Chocolate
Brownie Fudge Cake
• 84 •

Gilded Fleur de Sel
Caramel Cake
• 94 •

Chocolate Hazelnut
Gianduja Cake
• 86 •

Strawberry
Shortcake
• 96 •

Banana Chocolate
Fudge Cake
• 88 •

Tart Raspberry
Lemon Cake
• 98 •

"No Raisin"
Carrot Cake
• 90 •

Coconut Cake
with Passion Fruit Curd
• 100 •

CLASSIC VANILLA LAYER CAKE

Vanilla cake is the "plain white T-shirt" of the cake world: simple and classic, yet no two are created equal. Many of us have grown up accustomed to box-mix vanilla cake, which is light and, quite frankly, impossibly airy. Made-from-scratch vanilla cakes tend to be butter-based and are fairly heavy and rich. We tinkered for years to develop a recipe that would bridge the gap between the two, a cake rich in flavour but light in texture. This recipe achieves that beautifully—so much so that it serves as the base for all our vanilla cakes at the shops.

CAKE

4 cups all-purpose flour

4½ teaspoons baking powder

1 teaspoon salt

4 large eggs, room temperature

2 large egg whites, room temperature

1¾ cups unsalted butter, room temperature

2⅔ cups granulated sugar

1 tablespoon pure vanilla extract

2¼ cups whole milk, room temperature

CLASSIC VANILLA BUTTERCREAM

Prepare a double batch (page 222)

It is very important to not overbake this cake. It should be just turning a bit golden when it is ready. Test frequently with a toothpick when the baking time approaches 30 minutes.

It is also important not to overmix the batter, or the cake will lose its light texture.

1. Preheat the oven to 350°F. Grease three 9-inch round cake pans with butter or non-stick cooking spray, then line the bottoms with parchment paper.

2. In a medium bowl, whisk together the flour, baking powder and salt. In a small bowl, beat together the eggs and egg whites.

3. In the bowl of a stand mixer fitted with the paddle attachment, cream the butter and sugar on medium speed until light and fluffy, about 3 minutes. Add the eggs in 3 additions, beating well after each addition and stopping after each addition to scrape down the sides of the bowl. Add the vanilla and beat until well combined.

4. With the mixer on low speed, alternate adding the flour mixture in 3 additions and the milk in 2 additions, beginning and ending with the flour mixture. Blend after each addition until just combined, stopping the mixer to scrape down the sides of the bowl at least once. Divide the batter evenly between the pans, using a rubber spatula to spread it to the edges.

5. Bake for 30 minutes or until the tops are just turning a bit golden and a toothpick inserted in the centre comes out clean. For even baking, rotate the pans front to back halfway through. Allow the cakes to cool in the pans for 10 minutes before turning them out onto a wire rack to cool completely. Gently remove the parchment if it sticks to the bottom of the cakes.

6. Follow the instructions on page 215 to fill and assemble the cake. The finished cake should be enjoyed at room temperature, but may be covered and stored in the fridge for up to 4 days.

DARK CHOCOLATE BROWNIE FUDGE CAKE

There are people who love chocolate and there are people for whom chocolate is a way of life. We have created this cake for serious chocolate lovers. We believe the secret to ultimate chocolate satisfaction is layering, so we've filled rich chocolate cake layers with extra-dark chocolate fudge frosting, masked it in chocolate buttercream and topped it with big chocolate brownie chunks and dark chocolate ganache glaze. If you or someone you love is a chocolate addict, this recipe is our gift to you. Enjoy.

CAKE

3 large eggs, room temperature

1½ cups buttermilk, room temperature

1½ cups hot brewed coffee (instant or drip)

¾ cup vegetable oil

1½ teaspoons pure vanilla extract

3 cups all-purpose flour

3 cups granulated sugar

½ cup cocoa powder

1 tablespoon baking soda

1½ teaspoons baking powder

1½ teaspoons salt

DARK CHOCOLATE FUDGE FROSTING

Prepare 1 batch (page 231)

CHOCOLATE BUTTERCREAM

Prepare ½ batch (page 223)

CHOCOLATE GLAZE

Prepare ½ batch (page 239)

CHOCOLATE BROWNIE GARNISH

Prepare ½ batch of Death by Chocolate Brownies (page 50)

1. Preheat the oven to 350°F. Grease three 9-inch round cake pans with butter or non-stick cooking spray, then line the bottoms with parchment paper.

2. In a medium bowl, whisk together the eggs, buttermilk, hot coffee, vegetable oil and vanilla.

3. Before you place the bowl of a stand mixer on the stand, combine in the bowl the flour, sugar, cocoa powder, baking soda, baking powder and salt and whisk together. Add the wet mixture to the dry mixture and whisk to incorporate the ingredients.

4. Fit the mixer with the paddle attachment, then beat the batter on medium-low speed for 2 minutes, until it is well combined and smooth. Do not overmix the batter by beating it on high speed. Divide the batter evenly between the pans.

5. Bake for 30 to 40 minutes or until a toothpick inserted in the centre comes out clean. For even baking, rotate the pans front to back halfway through. Allow the cakes to cool in the pans for 10 minutes before turning them out onto a wire rack to cool completely. Gently remove the parchment if it sticks to the bottom of the cakes.

6. Fill the cooled cake with the fudge frosting, following the filling instructions on page 215. Mask the outside of the cake with the buttercream, following the instructions on page 215. Chill the cake in the fridge for 15 minutes.

7. Pour most of the glaze on the centre of the top. Gently spread the glaze outward using a small offset spatula until it begins to seep over the edge of the cake. Garnish the top of the cake edge with chunks of brownie, then drizzle the tops with the remaining glaze. The finished cake should be enjoyed at room temperature, but may be covered and stored in the fridge for up to 1 week.

 Tip For a simpler but equally indulgent version, simply leave out the buttercream, brownies and glaze; double the fudge frosting recipe and mask and fill the cake with that.

CHOCOLATE HAZELNUT GIANDUJA CAKE

Before we opened our first bakery and were coming up with our line of retail cakes, we knew we wanted to create an ode to one of our favourite pairings, chocolate and hazelnut, particularly the mixture of hazelnut paste and chocolate known in Italy as gianduja. Here, three layers of moist chocolate cake are filled with a gianduja ganache and masked with chocolate hazelnut buttercream. Our favourite part is the mound of gianduja curls that garnishes the entire top of the cake.

CAKE

3 large eggs, room temperature

1½ cups buttermilk, room temperature

1½ cups hot brewed coffee (drip or instant)

¾ cup vegetable oil

1½ teaspoons pure vanilla extract

3 cups all-purpose flour

3 cups granulated sugar

½ cup cocoa powder

1 tablespoon baking soda

1½ teaspoons baking powder

1½ teaspoons salt

2 cups skinned toasted hazelnuts (page 12)

Block of gianduja (hazelnut chocolate), slightly warm, to make 1½ cups curls

CHOCOLATE HAZELNUT GANACHE

Prepare 1 batch (page 241)

CHOCOLATE HAZELNUT BUTTERCREAM

Prepare ½ batch (page 224)

1. Preheat the oven to 350°F. Grease three 9-inch round cake pans with butter or non-stick cooking spray, then line the bottoms with parchment paper.

2. In a medium bowl, whisk together the eggs, buttermilk, hot coffee, vegetable oil and vanilla.

3. Before you place the bowl of a stand mixer on the stand, combine in the bowl the flour, sugar, cocoa powder, baking soda, baking powder and salt and whisk together. Add the wet mixture to the dry mixture and whisk to incorporate the ingredients.

4. Fit the mixer with the paddle attachment, then beat the batter on medium-low speed for 2 minutes, until it is well combined and smooth. Do not overmix the batter by beating it on high speed. Divide the batter evenly between the pans.

5. Bake for 30 to 40 minutes or until a toothpick inserted in the centre comes out clean. For even baking, rotate the pans front to back halfway through. Allow the cakes to cool in the pans for 10 minutes before turning them out onto a wire rack to cool completely. Gently remove the parchment if it sticks to the bottom of the cakes.

6. Fill the cake with the ganache, following the instructions on page 215. Place the cake in the fridge to chill for 15 minutes.

7. While the cake is chilling, in a food processor, pulse the hazelnuts a few times to coarsely chop them. Transfer to a large bowl.

8. Mask the outside of the cake with the buttercream, following the instructions on page 215. Carefully lift the cake and place your hand under the cake board. Holding the cake over the bowl of hazelnuts and scoop up and gently press handfuls of nuts around the lower third of the cake, allowing excess nuts to fall back into the bowl.

9. If you were able to source a large slab of gianduja, hold the slab over the cake, hold a large metal round cookie cutter at a 45-degree angle near the top of the slab, apply slight pressure and run it down the block, letting the chocolate curls mound on the cake. Or use a vegetable peeler on a smaller piece of chocolate to create large flakes to sprinkle on the top of the cake. The finished cake should be enjoyed at room temperature, but may be covered and stored in the fridge for up to 1 week.

BANANA CHOCOLATE FUDGE CAKE

This is our number one groom's cake at the shop. As two women, we had never considered chocolate chip banana cake to be a particularly masculine dessert and we have often indulged in it ourselves. It was only upon assembling this cake that the connection became clear. Layers of dense chocolate chip banana cake filled with dark—and we mean dark—fudge frosting, masked in chocolate buttercream and topped with poured chocolate ganache. As it turns out, we had inadvertently created the dessert version of BBQ, an indulgence so decadent that a sense of pride comes with eating it.

CAKE

3⅔ cups all-purpose flour

2 teaspoons baking powder

2 teaspoons baking soda

3 cups mashed ripe bananas

2 cups + 2 tablespoons loosely packed brown sugar

4 large eggs

1⅔ cups vegetable oil

2 teaspoons salt

1½ cups whole milk, room temperature

1 cup chocolate chips

DARK CHOCOLATE FUDGE FROSTING

Prepare 1 batch (page 231)

CHOCOLATE BUTTERCREAM

Prepare ½ batch (page 223)

CHOCOLATE GLAZE

Prepare ½ batch (page 239)

GARNISH (OPTIONAL)

⅓ cup banana chips

⅓ cup chocolate chips

1. Preheat the oven to 350°F. Grease three 9-inch round cake pans with butter or non-stick cooking spray, then line the bottoms with parchment paper.

2. In a medium bowl, whisk together the flour, baking powder and baking soda.

3. In the bowl of a stand mixer fitted with the paddle attachment, beat the bananas and brown sugar on medium speed until the mixture resembles a paste, about 2 minutes. Beat in the eggs, oil and salt until well combined.

4. With the mixer on low speed, alternate adding the flour mixture in 3 additions and the milk in 2 additions, beginning and ending with the flour mixture. Blend after each addition until just combined, stopping the mixer to scrape down the sides of the bowl at least once. Remove the bowl from the mixer and stir in the chocolate chips by hand. Divide the batter evenly between the pans, using a rubber spatula to spread it to the edges.

5. Bake for 30 minutes or until a toothpick inserted in the centre comes out clean. For even baking, rotate the pans front to back halfway through. Allow the cakes to cool in the pans for 10 minutes before turning them out onto a wire rack to cool completely. Gently remove the parchment if it sticks to the bottom of the cakes.

6. Fill the cake with the fudge frosting, following the instructions on page 215. Mask the outside of the cake with the buttercream, following the instructions on page 215. Chill the cake in the fridge for 15 minutes.

7. Pour the chocolate glaze on the centre of the top of the cake. Gently spread the glaze outward using a small offset spatula until it begins to seep over the edge of the cake. Garnish the top edge of the cake with banana chips and chocolate chips. The finished cake should be enjoyed at room temperature, but may be covered and stored in the fridge for up to 1 week.

 Tip This recipe also works wonderfully as muffins or a loaf. No toppings necessary. Simply bake in the chosen vessel and adjust bake times as needed. We recommend doing a toothpick test at 25 minutes and subsequently every 5 minutes until it comes out clean.

"No Raisin"
CARROT CAKE

Carrot cake is one of those cakes with as many recipes as there are bakers, and each is heralded by somebody to be the absolute best. We are no different, for a few simple reasons. Our cake is incredibly moist without being too dense, it is flavourful with a nice balance of spices, and, being layered, it has just the right ratio of cream cheese filling to cake. More importantly, though, there are *no raisins*! We thought we were the only ones who always picked around the raisins with the fine motor dexterity of a surgeon, leaving a little pile of shrivelled fruit on the empty plate. As it turns out, we weren't alone. Often the first question customers ask about our carrot cake is whether it contains raisins. We have received many a thank-you upon answering no, so we took out the guesswork and renamed it "No Raisin" Carrot Cake.

CAKE

2⅔ cups all-purpose flour

2 teaspoons + rounded ½ teaspoon baking powder

2 teaspoons + rounded ½ teaspoon baking soda

1 teaspoon + rounded ¼ teaspoon salt

1 teaspoon + rounded ¼ teaspoon cinnamon

1 teaspoon nutmeg

2⅔ cups granulated sugar

2 cups vegetable oil

5 large eggs

4 cups finely grated peeled carrots (8 to 10 large carrots)

⅔ cup chopped pecans

CREAM CHEESE BUTTERCREAM

Prepare 1 batch (page 227)

Tip

Feel free to use our Cooked Cream Cheese Frosting on page 236 instead of the buttercream.

1. Preheat the oven to 350°F. Grease three 9-inch round cake pans with butter or non-stick cooking spray, then line the bottoms with parchment paper.

2. In a medium bowl, whisk together the flour, baking powder, baking soda, salt, cinnamon and nutmeg.

3. In the bowl of a stand mixer fitted with the paddle attachment, beat the sugar with the oil on medium speed until well combined. Add the eggs one at a time, beating for about 15 seconds after each addition. Stop the mixer to scrape down the sides of the bowl at least once.

4. With the mixer on low speed, add the flour mixture in 3 additions, mixing after each addition until just combined and stopping after each addition to scrape down the sides of the bowl. Do not overmix or the cake will not have a light texture. Remove the bowl from the mixer and stir in the carrots and pecans by hand. Divide the batter evenly between the pans, using a rubber spatula to spread it to the edges.

5. Bake for 35 to 40 minutes or until the tops are medium to dark golden brown and feel a bit springy to the touch; your finger should not leave an indent. (Unlike with most cakes, the clean-toothpick test will indicate the cake is done several minutes before it actually is.) For even baking, rotate the pans front to back halfway through. Allow the cakes to cool in the pans for 10 minutes before turning them out onto a wire rack to cool completely. Gently remove the parchment if it sticks to the bottom of the cakes.

6. Fill and mask the cake with the cream cheese buttercream, following the instructions on page 215. The finished cake should be enjoyed at room temperature, but may be covered and stored in the fridge for up to 1 week.

CARAMEL APPLE CAKE

We both remember as kids how the arrival of fall meant back to school, raking leaves, Thanksgiving—and caramel apples. It seemed almost impossible that our moms would allow such a yummy, decadent, candy-like confection. It must be the apple, we figured, and then giggled to ourselves, convinced that we had pulled one over on our moms. We get a lot of requests for caramel apple cake at the shops in the fall, and we're sure it has to do with that delicious balance of decadence from the caramel and comforting heartiness from the apple cake. Our version features moist apple spice cake, a filling of caramel frosting made with brown sugar and a garnish of traditional poured caramel.

CAKE

3⅓ cups all-purpose flour

1¾ teaspoons baking powder

Rounded ½ teaspoon baking soda

Rounded ½ teaspoon salt

1¼ teaspoons cinnamon

Rounded ¼ teaspoon ground ginger

Rounded ¼ teaspoon nutmeg

Rounded ¼ teaspoon ground allspice

1¼ cups unsweetened applesauce

½ cup plain yogurt

1½ teaspoons pure vanilla extract

2½ cups granulated sugar

¾ cup + 2 tablespoons unsalted butter, room temperature

4 large eggs

1 cup finely chopped walnuts

1 green apple, peeled, cored, finely chopped

CARAMEL FROSTING

Prepare 1 batch (page 232)

SALTED CARAMEL SAUCE (OPTIONAL)

Prepare 1 batch (page 190)

1. Preheat the oven to 350°F. Grease three 9-inch round cake pans with butter or non-stick cooking spray, then line the bottoms with parchment paper.

2. In a medium bowl, whisk together the flour, baking powder, baking soda, salt, cinnamon, ginger, nutmeg and allspice. In a separate bowl, stir together the applesauce, yogurt and vanilla.

3. In the bowl of a stand mixer fitted with the paddle attachment, cream the sugar and butter on medium speed until light and fluffy, about 3 minutes. Beat in the eggs one at a time, beating well after each addition and stopping to scrape down the sides of the bowl before adding the next egg. Add the applesauce mixture and beat well.

4. With the mixer on low speed, slowly add the flour mixture to the creamed butter mixture, blending just until incorporated and stopping once to scrape down the sides of the bowl. Remove the bowl from the mixer and gently fold in the walnuts and apple. Divide the batter evenly between the pans and smooth with a small offset spatula to ensure the cakes bake evenly.

5. Bake for 30 minutes or until a toothpick inserted in the centre comes out clean. For even baking, rotate the pans front to back halfway through. Allow the cakes to cool in the pans for 10 minutes before turning them out onto a wire rack to cool completely. Gently remove the parchment if it sticks to the bottom of the cakes.

6. Frost and assemble the cake, following the instructions on page 215. Drizzle with the caramel sauce, if desired. The finished cake should be enjoyed at room temperature, but may be covered and stored in the fridge for up to 6 days.

Tip In its completed form this cake is sweet and decadent, but the apple cake base is also wonderful on its own in muffin form. Simply line a muffin tin with cupcake liners and fill each liner three-quarters full. Bake at 350°F for 20 to 25 minutes or until a toothpick comes out clean.

Gilded Fleur de Sel
CARAMEL CAKE

Desserts with fleur de sel caramel are often paired with chocolate, but the true flavour of the caramel really shines when it takes centre stage. Here we pair it with a simple vanilla cake, which provides the perfect canvas for the rich, buttery caramel. Toffee pieces not only add another dimension of caramel flavour but also provide a nice crunch. The pièce de résistance is the edible gold leaf, which "gilds" the cake and sets off the golden colour of the caramel.

CAKE

4 cups all-purpose flour

4½ teaspoons baking powder

1 teaspoon salt

4 large eggs, room temperature

2 large egg whites, room temperature

1¾ cups unsalted butter, room temperature

2⅔ cups granulated sugar

1 tablespoon pure vanilla extract

2¼ cups whole milk, room temperature

SALTED CARAMEL BUTTERCREAM

Prepare 1 batch (page 225). Reserve ½ cup of the salted caramel sauce to garnish the finished cake.

ENGLISH TOFFEE WITH TOASTED ALMONDS

Prepare ½ batch (page 194)

GARNISH

½ cup Salted Caramel Sauce (page 190)

Edible gold leaf (see source guide, page 248)

1. Preheat the oven to 350°F. Grease three 9-inch round cake pans with butter or non-stick cooking spray, then line the bottoms with parchment paper.

2. In a large bowl, whisk together the flour, baking powder and salt. In a separate bowl, beat together the eggs and egg whites.

3. In the bowl of a stand mixer fitted with the paddle attachment, cream the butter and sugar on medium speed until light and fluffy, about 3 minutes. With the mixer on medium speed, add the eggs in 3 additions, beating well after each addition and stopping after each addition to scrape down the sides of the bowl. Add the vanilla and beat until well combined.

4. With the mixer on low speed, alternate adding the flour mixture in 3 additions and the milk in 2 additions, beginning and ending with the flour mixture. Blend after each addition until just combined, stopping the mixer to scrape down the sides of the bowl at least once. Divide the batter evenly between the pans, using a rubber spatula to spread it to the edges.

5. Bake for 30 minutes or until a toothpick inserted in the centre comes out clean. For even baking, rotate the pans front to back halfway through. Allow the cakes to cool in the pans for 10 minutes before turning them out onto a wire rack to cool completely. Gently remove the parchment if it sticks to the bottom of the cakes.

6. Fill and mask the cake with the buttercream, following the instructions on page 215. Break the English toffee into pieces and garnish the top of the cake. Drizzle the salted caramel sauce over the entire top of the cake. Finish the cake with a sprinkle of edible gold leaf. The finished cake should be enjoyed at room temperature, but may be covered and stored in the fridge for up to 4 days.

 Tip If you're tight on time go ahead and use a store-bought English toffee.

STRAWBERRY SHORTCAKE

Strawberry shortcake is often made with angel food cake, but we use a chiffon cake to provide more stability for layering. Chiffon cakes are light and airy because meringue is folded into the batter. The process is a bit time consuming, but well worth the added effort. Using only egg whites keeps the cake the white colour that most people associate with a shortcake.

CAKE

3¾ cups cake and pastry flour

1 tablespoon + ¾ teaspoon baking powder

Rounded ½ teaspoon salt

1¾ cups whole milk, room temperature

1¼ teaspoons pure vanilla extract

1¼ cups + 2 tablespoons unsalted butter, room temperature

2½ cups granulated sugar (reserve ⅓ cup)

9 large egg whites, room temperature

2 pints fresh strawberries, 8 or 10 reserved for garnish, the remainder hulled and sliced

MASCARPONE CREAM

Prepare 1 batch (page 242)

Tip

This style of cake is known as a "naked" cake because the sides are left bare. Exposure to air can dry out a cake, so this style works best with cakes that, like this chiffon cake, have a short shelf life and should be eaten the same day they are made.

1. Preheat the oven to 350°F. Lightly grease three 9-inch round cake pans with butter or non-stick cooking spray, then line the bottoms with parchment paper.

2. In a medium bowl, whisk together the flour, baking powder and salt. In a large measuring cup, combine the milk and vanilla.

3. In the bowl of a stand mixer fitted with the paddle attachment, cream the butter and 2 cups plus 3 tablespoons of the sugar on medium speed until light and fluffy, about 3 minutes.

4. With the mixer on low speed, alternate adding the flour mixture in 3 additions and the milk mixture in 2 additions, beginning and ending with the flour mixture. Blend after each addition until just combined, stopping the mixer to scrape down the sides of the bowl at least once. Scrape the batter into the large bowl and set aside.

5. Thoroughly clean and dry the mixer bowl. Using the whisk attachment, whisk the egg whites on medium-high speed until soft peaks form, 2 to 3 minutes. Add the reserved ⅓ cup of sugar in a slow, thin, even stream. Continue to whisk on medium-high speed until the meringue is glossy and holds stiff peaks.

6. Gently fold a bit of the meringue into the batter to lighten it. Gently but thoroughly fold in the remaining meringue, being careful to not overmix the batter or it will deflate. Divide the batter evenly between the pans and smooth the tops with an offset spatula or the back of a spoon.

7. Bake for 30 to 40 minutes or until a toothpick inserted in the centre comes out clean. For even baking, rotate the pans front to back halfway through. Allow the cakes to cool in the pans for 10 minutes before turning them out onto a wire rack to cool completely. Gently remove the parchment if it sticks to the bottom of the cakes.

8. Spoon about a third of the mascarpone cream on the first layer of the cake. Using an offset spatula, spread it out to the edges and slightly over in some places. The cream should be at least ½-inch thick. Arrange half of the sliced strawberries evenly over the top. Place the next layer of cake over the berries. Repeat layering with a third of the mascarpone cream and the remaining sliced strawberries, then cover with the final layer of cake. Cover the top cake layer with the remaining mascarpone cream, spreading it evenly. Garnish the top of the cake with the reserved strawberries, whole or cut in half. The finished cake should be covered and stored in the fridge and enjoyed slightly chilled the same day.

TART RASPBERRY LEMON CAKE

Lemon cake has always been a popular selection for weddings and special events. Lemon appeals to most palates, but it can also be a little boring at times. We wanted to create a cake that would elevate all the best elements of a traditional lemon cake while adding something that would take it to the next level. Lemon cake's flavour typically comes from lemon juice and zest, but once baked the cake lacks the wonderful tartness of fresh lemons. We add fresh lemon juice to a raspberry buttercream to create a more stimulating flavour. The result is a cake that will please just about everybody, and is interesting and beautiful enough to serve at a special event.

CAKE

3 cups cake and pastry flour

1 rounded teaspoon baking soda

1 cup + 2 tablespoons unsalted butter, room temperature

3 cups granulated sugar (reserve ⅓ cup)

9 large eggs, separated, room temperature

1 cup + 2 tablespoons sour cream

2 tablespoons + 1 teaspoon lemon zest

½ cup fresh lemon juice

4½ teaspoons pure vanilla extract

RASPBERRY BUTTERCREAM

Prepare 1 batch (page 228), adding ½ cup fresh lemon juice at the same time as the vanilla

Tip

To create the mini cakes in the photo, bake the cake in two 9-inch square pans. Once cooled, use a 2- to 2½-inch round cutter to cut out an even number of cake rounds. Fill and mask using the same method you would for the larger cake. To create the decorative flower topper, follow the flower piping instructions on page 219.

1. Preheat the oven to 350°F. Grease three 9-inch round cake pans with butter or non-stick cooking spray, then line the bottoms with parchment paper.

2. In a large bowl, whisk together the flour and baking soda.

3. In the bowl of a stand mixer fitted with the paddle attachment, cream the butter and 2⅔ cups of the sugar on medium speed until light and fluffy, about 3 minutes. Add the egg yolks one at a time, beating well after each addition. Scrape down the sides of the bowl. Add the sour cream, lemon zest, lemon juice and vanilla. Beat until combined.

4. With the mixer on low speed, add the flour mixture in 3 additions, beating after each addition until combined. Stop to scrape down the sides of the bowl as needed. Transfer the batter to a large bowl and set aside.

5. Thoroughly clean and dry the mixer bowl. Using the whisk attachment, whisk the egg whites on medium-high speed until soft peaks form, 2 to 3 minutes. Add the reserved ⅓ cup of sugar in a slow, thin, even stream. Continue to whisk on medium-high speed until the meringue is glossy and holds stiff peaks.

6. Gently fold a bit of the meringue into the batter to lighten it. Gently but thoroughly fold in the remaining meringue, being careful to not overmix the batter or it will deflate. Divide the batter evenly between the pans and smooth the tops with an offset spatula or the back of a spoon.

7. Bake for 30 to 35 minutes or until a toothpick inserted in the centre comes out clean. For even baking, rotate the pans front to back halfway through. Allow the cakes to cool in the pans for 10 minutes before turning them out onto a wire rack to cool completely. Gently remove the parchment if it sticks to the bottom of the cakes.

8. Fill and mask the cake with the buttercream, following the instructions on page 215. The cake should be enjoyed at room temperature, but may be covered and stored in the fridge for up to 6 days.

COCONUT CAKE
with Passion Fruit Curd

Passion fruit is a flavour that many people are not familiar with, but those who know it love it. It is very tart, much like lemon or lime, but also has an unmistakable flavour. Because of the tartness, it is perfectly paired with the richness of coconut cake. The toasted coconut on the outside lends to the tropical feel and provides a delicious nuttiness.

COCONUT CAKE

2½ cups all-purpose flour

2 teaspoons baking powder

½ teaspoon baking soda

½ teaspoon salt

¾ cup coconut milk

¾ cup buttermilk, room temperature

¾ cup unsalted butter, room temperature

1¾ cups granulated sugar (reserve ¼ cup)

6 large eggs, separated, room temperature

2½ teaspoons coconut extract

1 teaspoon pure vanilla extract

½ teaspoon cream of tartar

PASSION FRUIT CURD

Prepare 1 batch (page 246)

7-MINUTE MERINGUE FROSTING

Prepare 1 batch (page 237) once the cakes have cooled

GARNISH

½ cup shredded coconut, lightly toasted in a frying pan

1. Preheat the oven to 350°F. Grease three 9-inch round cake pans with butter or non-stick cooking spray, then line the bottoms with parchment paper.

2. In a medium bowl, whisk together the flour, baking powder, baking soda and salt. In a large measuring cup, combine the coconut milk and buttermilk.

3. In the bowl of a stand mixer fitted with the paddle attachment, cream the butter and 1½ cups of the sugar on medium speed until light and fluffy, about 3 minutes. Add the egg yolks one at a time, beating well after each addition. Scrape down the sides of the bowl. Add the coconut extract and vanilla and beat until combined.

4. With the mixer on low speed, alternate adding the flour mixture in 3 additions and the buttermilk mixture in 2 additions, beginning and ending with the flour mixture. Scrape the batter into a large bowl and set aside.

5. Thoroughly clean and dry the mixer bowl. Using the whisk attachment, whisk the egg whites on medium speed for 1 minute. Add the cream of tartar and whisk on medium-high speed until soft peaks form, about 5 minutes. Add the reserved ¼ cup of sugar in a slow, thin, even stream. Continue to whisk on medium-high speed until the meringue is glossy and holds stiff peaks.

6. Gently fold a bit of the meringue into the batter to lighten it. Gently but thoroughly fold in the remaining meringue, being careful to not overmix the batter or it will deflate. Divide the batter evenly between the pans and smooth the tops with an offset spatula or the back of a spoon.

7. Bake for 35 to 40 minutes or until a toothpick inserted in the centre comes out clean. For even baking, rotate the pans front to back halfway through. Allow the cakes to cool in the pans for 10 minutes before turning them out onto a wire rack to cool completely. Gently remove the parchment if it sticks to the bottom of the cakes.

8. Once the cakes have cooled, make the frosting. Fill the cakes with the passion fruit curd, following the instructions on page 215, noting the technique for filling with a curd in step 2. Mask the outside of the cake with the frosting in a rustic style, following the "Rustic Finish" variation on page 217. Garnish the top of the cake with the coconut. The finished cake should be enjoyed chilled because the filling is not stable at room temperature. Cover and store in the fridge for up to 3 days.

4

LOAVES
SCONES
BUNDTS
AND TORTES

APPLE CINNAMON COFFEE CAKE

The name "coffee cake" is a bit of a misnomer, in that it often doesn't contain coffee at all. Traditionally, coffee cake is a single-layer cake or loaf that is made to be eaten with coffee or as part of a coffee break. It lies somewhere between a cake and a muffin and comes in a wide variety of flavours. We knew we wanted to include a coffee cake in the book because it is emblematic of the type of home-baked North American desserts that we feel passionate about. In our mind, the key to a great coffee cake is a light white cake, a good blend of spices and plenty of streusel topping. We tossed in some apple for added flavour and some acidity to balance the sweetness.

CAKE

1½ cups all-purpose flour

1½ teaspoons baking powder

⅛ teaspoon salt

1 cup sour cream

1 teaspoon baking soda

½ cup unsalted butter, room temperature

1 cup granulated sugar

2 large eggs

1 teaspoon pure vanilla extract

STREUSEL FILLING

2 green apples, peeled, cored and diced into ½-inch pieces

1 tablespoon lemon juice

⅔ cup packed brown sugar

½ cup all-purpose flour

½ cup quick-cooking rolled oats

½ teaspoon cinnamon

¼ teaspoon salt

6 tablespoons cold unsalted butter, cut into small pieces

½ cup chopped pecans

1. Preheat the oven to 350°F. Grease a 9- × 5-inch loaf pan with butter or non-stick cooking spray. Line the bottom with parchment paper.

2. To make the cake, in a small bowl, whisk together the flour, baking powder and salt. In a small bowl, stir together the sour cream and baking soda.

3. In the bowl of a stand mixer fitted with the paddle attachment, cream the butter and sugar on medium speed until light and fluffy, about 3 minutes. Add the eggs one at a time, beating well after each addition. Add the vanilla and mix until combined.

4. With the mixer on low speed, alternate adding the flour mixture in 3 additions and the sour cream mixture in 2 additions, beginning and ending with the flour mixture. Increase the speed to medium and beat until just combined. Stop to scrape down the sides of the bowl, then mix for another 15 seconds.

5. To make the streusel filling, toss the apples with lemon juice. Set aside.

6. In a large bowl, mix together the brown sugar, flour, oats, cinnamon and salt. Add the butter pieces and mix with your hands until the butter is combined, the mixture has the texture of coarse meal and small chunks of streusel form. Be careful to not overmix or it will form a dough. Add the diced apples and mix by hand so they are coated in streusel topping.

7. Spoon half of the cake batter into the lined pan. It will not spread smoothly, so place dollops of batter all over the bottom of the pan and then gently spread and smooth them with the back of a spoon. Evenly sprinkle two-thirds of the streusel filling over the batter, then dollop the remaining batter over the streusel. Sprinkle with the remaining streusel topping and the pecans.

8. Bake for 45 to 50 minutes or until a toothpick inserted in the centre comes out clean. For even baking, rotate the pan front to back halfway through. Allow the loaf to cool completely before removing from the pan and slicing it. The loaf can be stored in an airtight container for up to 1 week.

LEMON TEA CAKES

It can sometimes seem hard to find the value in taking time to make a homemade gift, but we feel most people would agree that receiving a homemade treat is always a pleasure. We think the key to successful edible gift giving is baking a treat that most people will enjoy, that is fairly simple to make and that provides the opportunity to get creative with the packaging. This lemon tea cake meets those criteria perfectly. As a bonus, it also bakes up beautifully as a lemon Bundt cake.

TEA CAKES

3 cups all-purpose flour

1 teaspoon salt

½ teaspoon baking powder

½ teaspoon baking soda

¾ cup buttermilk, room temperature

¼ cup fresh lemon juice

1 teaspoon pure vanilla extract

1 cup unsalted butter, room temperature

2 cups granulated sugar

4 large eggs, room temperature

⅓ cup lemon zest (from 6 to 8 lemons)

LEMON GLAZE

2 cups icing sugar, sifted

¼ cup fresh lemon juice

2 tablespoons 35% cream

1 teaspoon unsalted butter, melted

⅛ teaspoon salt

1. Preheat the oven to 350°F. Grease 8 to 10 small loaf pans or 14 to 16 mini loaf pans with butter or non-stick cooking spray. Lightly flour the pans, tapping out any excess. Arrange the loaf pans on a baking sheet.

2. To make the tea cakes, in a medium bowl, whisk together the flour, salt, baking powder and baking soda. Measure the buttermilk into a measuring cup, then stir in the lemon juice and vanilla.

3. In the bowl of a stand mixer fitted with the paddle attachment, cream the butter and sugar on medium speed until light and fluffy, about 3 minutes. Add the eggs one at a time, beating well after each addition. Beat in the lemon zest. Stop the mixer and scrape down the sides of the bowl.

4. With the mixer on medium speed, alternate adding the flour mixture in 3 additions and the buttermilk mixture in 2 additions, beginning and ending with the flour mixture. Blend after each addition until just combined. Stop to scrape down the sides of the bowl, then mix for another 15 seconds. Pour the batter into the Bundt pan or evenly divide between the loaf pans, filling three-quarters full. Smooth the tops.

5. Bake the mini loaves for 20 to 35 minutes or the small loaves for 30 to 35 minutes, until a toothpick inserted in the centre comes out clean. For even baking, rotate the baking sheet front to back halfway through. Transfer the pans to a wire rack and allow the loaves to cool completely before removing from the pans.

6. To make the lemon glaze, whisk together all the ingredients in a small bowl until perfectly smooth. Spread the tops of the cooled tea cakes with the glaze and allow them to sit for 30 minutes to set. The tea cakes can be stored in an airtight container for up to 1 week.

 Tip If you intend to package the loaves and give them as gifts, we recommend brushing the tops with a syrup of 1 part lemon juice to 2 parts sugar before applying the glaze. This will keep them moist for a longer period.

BLUEBERRY SCONES
with Clotted Cream

We never guessed when we opened our first shop that our blueberry scones would become a signature item. When we opened in 2010 we started out baking 12 scones each morning. Today we bake upwards of 200 on some mornings. Homemade clotted cream—35% cream that has been reduced over heat and then whipped—certainly adds to the appeal, but it is the scone itself that keeps people coming back. As with several of our most popular recipes, this was Allyson's Nana's recipe. Keep in mind that it is a gentle touch that leads to a truly tender scone. The key is blending by hand rather than in a mixer or food processor, using cold hands, and most important, not overmixing. And be sure your blueberries are fully frozen so they won't "bleed" too much when they're mixed in.

SCONES

2 cups all-purpose flour

⅓ cup + 1 tablespoon granulated sugar

4 teaspoons baking powder

¼ teaspoon cream of tartar

¼ teaspoon salt

½ cup cold unsalted butter, cut into pieces

1 large egg

½ cup + 2 teaspoons whole milk

1 cup fully frozen wild blueberries

EGG WASH

1 large egg

1 tablespoon water

GARNISH

2 tablespoons coarse sugar

CLOTTED CREAM

4 cups 35% cream

1. Preheat the oven to 350°F. Line a baking sheet with parchment paper.

2. To make the scones, in a large bowl, whisk together the flour, sugar, baking powder, cream of tartar and salt. Blend the butter into the flour mixture with a pastry cutter. The mixture should look like a coarse meal.

3. In a small bowl, beat together the milk and egg with a fork. Slowly add to the flour mixture and blend together with your hands just until the dough comes together. You should be able to separate the dough into individual pieces, and there may still be some small pieces of butter visible.

4. Add the frozen blueberries and incorporate them by hand, being careful not to overwork the dough. Separate the dough into 6 even pieces, gently shape each piece into a round clump of dough and arrange on the lined baking sheet.

5. In a small bowl, beat together the egg and water with a fork, then brush the tops of the scones with the egg wash. Sprinkle with coarse sugar.

6. Bake for 30 minutes or until the tops are a light golden colour. For even baking, rotate the baking sheet front to back halfway through. Transfer the scones to a wire rack to cool completely. The scones can be stored in an airtight container for up to 3 days.

7. To make the clotted cream, in a large, heavy saucepan, bring the cream to a boil over medium-high heat. Immediately reduce the heat to low and simmer the cream, stirring occasionally, for 45 to 50 minutes or until it has reduced by half, has thickened and is a creamy ivory colour. Pour it into an airtight container and chill in the fridge for at least 4 hours.

8. Pour the chilled cream into the bowl of a stand mixer fitted with the whisk attachment. Whip on medium speed until the cream just holds medium-soft peaks. Take care not to overwhip the cream or it will turn into chunks of butter. The clotted cream can be stored in an airtight container in the fridge for up to 1 week.

SHARP CHEDDAR AND CHIVE SCONES

Scones, much like croissants, are one of the rare pastries that work equally well in savoury as sweet form. Sharp cheddar and chives make these scones appealing to most palates, and they pair wonderfully with soups to make a hearty meal. As with the sweet version, a delicate touch when mixing is advised to ensure tenderness. The inclination is to knead until all the ingredients are completely blended, but the best result is achieved by cutting the ingredients together by hand or with a pastry cutter until the dough barely forms a single mass. Any small bits of butter that were not fully blended in will melt and distribute themselves during baking.

SCONES

3 cups all-purpose flour

1 tablespoon granulated sugar

1 tablespoon baking powder

1 teaspoon salt

1½ cups coarsely grated extra-sharp cheddar cheese, plus more for garnish

½ cup finely chopped chives

2¼ cups 35% cream

EGG WASH

1 large egg

1 tablespoon water

Tip

Play around with the type of cheese you use. Strong-flavoured hard cheeses like Parmesan and Asiago work very well, as do white cheddar and combinations of several cheeses.

1. Preheat the oven to 350°F. Line a baking sheet with parchment paper.

2. In a large bowl, whisk together the flour, sugar, baking powder and salt. Add the cheddar and chives and stir to combine. Add the cream, mixing with a fork just until a sticky dough forms. Use your hands to bring the dough together, mixing only to the point that the dough forms a ball.

3. Separate the dough into 8 even pieces, gently shape each piece into a round clump of dough and arrange on the lined baking sheet.

4. In a small bowl, beat together the egg and water with a fork, then brush the tops of the scones with the egg wash. Sprinkle with a bit more grated cheddar.

5. Bake for 30 minutes or until the tops are a light golden colour. For even baking, rotate the baking sheet front to back halfway through. Transfer the scones to a wire rack to cool completely. The scones can be stored in an airtight container for up to 3 days.

STICKY TOFFEE PUDDING
with Hot Bourbon Toffee Sauce

For most people, sticky toffee pudding conjures thoughts of winter, the English countryside and maybe a fondness for Dickens. Our moist, spiced date pudding covered in homemade bourbon caramel sauce is the perfect cold-weather dessert. We serve it year round at the shops because it is a customer favourite regardless of the temperature outside. We think the reason is twofold: our version is lighter in texture than most, so it doesn't feel out of place in warmer months, and it falls under the category of what we call "comfort desserts" because it has the added benefit of making you feel a little bit better instead of just a little bit fuller.

PUDDING

1¼ cups chopped pitted dates

1 cup water

1 teaspoon instant coffee granules

¼ cup hot water

2 cups all-purpose flour

4½ teaspoons baking soda

2¾ teaspoons baking powder

1 teaspoon cinnamon

½ teaspoon ground ginger

¼ teaspoon nutmeg

⅓ cup unsalted butter, room temperature

1 cup granulated sugar

¼ cup loosely packed brown sugar

3 large eggs

BOURBON TOFFEE SAUCE

1¼ cups unsalted butter

1⅔ cups loosely packed brown sugar

1¼ cups 35% cream

2 tablespoons bourbon

1½ teaspoons pure vanilla extract

1. Preheat the oven to 350°F. Grease a 9-inch square baking pan or twelve 6-ounce ramekins with butter or non-stick cooking spray. Arrange ramekins on a baking sheet.

2. To make the pudding, in a medium saucepan, combine the dates and 1 cup water. Cook over medium heat until the dates have softened and the water has evaporated, about 8 minutes. Mix the instant coffee with ¼ cup hot water and add it to the dates. Continue cooking until all the liquid is gone. Set aside to cool.

3. In a medium bowl, whisk together the flour, baking soda, baking powder, cinnamon, ginger and nutmeg.

4. In the bowl of a stand mixer fitted with the paddle attachment, cream the butter, granulated sugar and brown sugar on medium speed until light and fluffy, about 3 minutes. Add the eggs one at a time, beating well after each addition. Stir in the cooled date mixture.

5. With the mixer on medium speed, add the flour mixture to the creamed butter and date mixture in 3 additions, mixing until just combined and stopping to scrape down the sides of the bowl at least once. Pour the batter into the prepared pan or fill individual ramekins two-thirds full.

6. Bake the ramekins for 20 minutes or the large pudding for 30 to 40 minutes or until a toothpick inserted in the centre comes out clean. For even baking, rotate the baking sheet front to back halfway through. Allow the pudding to cool slightly.

7. To make the bourbon toffee sauce, in a small saucepan, melt the butter over medium heat. Add the brown sugar and cream and continue cooking, stirring occasionally, until the sugar is fully dissolved. Bring to a boil and cook, stirring, until the sauce is slightly thickened. Remove from the heat and stir in the bourbon and vanilla.

8. Poke the tops of the baked pudding with a skewer and pour the sauce over the top, reserving some for serving. The pudding can be stored in an airtight container for up to 5 days. Reheat the sauce and pudding in the microwave until hot.

CARAMEL APPLE BREAD PUDDING

Food waste is a huge problem for food-based businesses, and as a small business owner, it can sometimes feel like you need a statistics degree to figure out exactly how much of anything to make for any given day. Even with all the best efforts, though, leftovers are unavoidable, and one of the best ways to deal with them is to find ways to use them. In our case this led to a very happy accident. Bread pudding makes good use of excess egg yolks and also works best with day-old croissants. For us, it was a great way to reduce waste, but for customers it was simply a delicious dessert. So much so that we now bake croissants specifically to use in the bread pudding.

APPLE FILLING

6 apples, peeled, cored and sliced ¼-inch thick

⅓ cup maple syrup

⅓ cup loosely packed brown sugar

2 tablespoons unsalted butter

PUDDING

7 large egg yolks

1⅔ cups 35% cream

1⅔ cups whole milk

⅔ cup loosely packed brown sugar

¾ teaspoon cinnamon

¼ teaspoon salt

1 teaspoon pure vanilla extract

10 day-old croissants, cut into ½ inch cubes

⅔ cup pecans, chopped and toasted (page 12)

SALTED CARAMEL SAUCE

Prepare 1 batch (page 190)

1. Preheat the oven to 300°F. Lightly grease a 10-inch square baking pan or twelve 6-ounce ramekins with butter or non-stick cooking spray. Arrange the ramekins on a baking sheet.

2. To make the apple filling, combine the apples, maple syrup, brown sugar and butter in a large pot and cook over low heat, stirring occasionally, until the apples are tender, about 10 minutes. Do not overcook the apples or they will become mushy. Transfer the apples to a large bowl and set aside.

3. Meanwhile, make the custard for the pudding. In a large bowl, whisk together the egg yolks. Add the cream, milk, brown sugar, cinnamon, salt and vanilla. Whisk until well combined.

4. Add the croissant cubes and toasted pecans to the apples. Toss until combined, then scrape the mixture into the prepared pan or ramekins. Pour the custard over the top of the croissant mixture and let sit for 10 minutes to allow the croissants to soak up the custard.

5. If using a baking pan, cover the pan with tin foil and bake for 45 minutes. Remove the foil, increase the oven temperature to 325°F and bake for another 10 to 15 minutes or until the top is golden and the pudding is fully set. If using ramekins, arrange on a baking sheet, cover with tin foil and bake for 25 minutes. Remove the foil, increase the oven temperature to 325°F and bake for another 5 to 10 minutes or until the tops are golden and the puddings are fully set. Allow to cool slightly before serving.

6. Drizzle with the caramel sauce before serving. More sauce can be added once plated and served.

 Tip As with most apple recipes, this bread pudding is delicious served with vanilla ice cream or Crème Anglaise (page 244).

WINTER CRANBERRY PUDDING

An extremely moist cake-like pudding studded with cranberries, it is a light version of traditional dark steamed Christmas pudding. The contrast of the sweet brown sugar sauce and the tart cranberries is nothing short of addictive.

PUDDING

2 cups + 2 tablespoons all-purpose flour

2 teaspoons baking powder

Pinch of salt

½ cup orange juice

½ cup water

1 teaspoon pure vanilla extract

½ cup unsalted butter, room temperature

1 cup granulated sugar

2 large eggs, room temperature

3 cups fresh or frozen cranberries

BROWN SUGAR SAUCE

1 cup packed brown sugar

1 tablespoon all-purpose flour

½ cup water

½ cup 35% cream

1 tablespoon unsalted butter

Tip

Once you have been successful with this recipe and using the *bain marie* (water bath), go ahead and try baking it in different vessels such as the mini Bundt pans we used in the photo.

1. Preheat the oven to 350°F. Grease a 9-inch springform pan with butter or non-stick cooking spray. To make the pan watertight, wrap the outside in tin foil. Place the pan inside a larger baking pan or roasting pan. Fashion a tin foil tent that will form a complete seal over the larger pan.

2. To make the pudding, in a medium bowl, whisk together 2 cups of the flour, the baking powder and salt. In a measuring cup, stir together the orange juice, water and vanilla.

3. In the bowl of a stand mixer fitted with the paddle attachment, cream the butter and sugar on medium speed until light and fluffy, about 3 minutes. Add the eggs one at a time, beating well after each addition.

4. With the mixer on medium speed, slowly add the orange juice mixture to the creamed butter mixture. The batter will look curdled, which is normal.

5. With the mixer on medium-low speed, add the flour mixture to the batter ½ cup at a time, blending well after each addition and stopping the mixer after each addition to scrape down the sides of the bowl.

6. In the bowl you used for the flour, gently toss the frozen cranberries with the remaining 2 tablespoons of flour. (This will prevent the cranberries from "bleeding" into the batter.) Gently fold the berries into the batter. Spread the batter in the springform pan.

7. Place the pan in the oven. Pour boiling water into the larger pan to come halfway up the side of the springform pans. Cover with the foil tent and crimp the edges to seal well.

8. Bake for 1 hour or until the pudding is set and a toothpick inserted in the centre comes out clean. Wearing oven mitts, remove the pudding from the water and allow it to cool for 10 minutes. (Turn off the oven and let the water bath cool completely so there is no risk of scalding yourself when removing it.)

9. Make the brown sugar sauce while the pudding cools. In a small saucepan, whisk together the brown sugar and flour. Add the water, cream and butter. Bring to a boil over medium-high heat and cook until the sauce thickens, about 3 minutes. Remove from the heat.

10. Remove the sides of the springform pan. Portion the warm pudding into dessert bowls and pour the hot sauce over it. Any leftover sauce and steamed pudding can be stored separately in airtight containers in the fridge for up to 3 days.

CINNAMON PULL-APART BREAD

Our cinnamon pull-apart bread is like a cinnamon bun double whammy. There is something about all those visible layers of butter, brown sugar and cinnamon sandwiched between soft, caramelized dough bursting out of the loaf pan with the scent of cinnamon that makes you want to dig in there, rip it apart and eat to your heart's content.

CINNAMON BREAD

2¾ cups + 1 tablespoon all-purpose flour

¼ cup granulated sugar

2¼ teaspoons instant yeast (1 envelope)

½ teaspoon salt

4 tablespoons unsalted butter

⅓ cup whole milk

¼ cup water

1 teaspoon pure vanilla extract

2 large eggs, room temperature

CINNAMON SUGAR FILLING

1 cup loosely packed brown sugar (more if needed)

2 teaspoons cinnamon (more if needed)

½ cup unsalted butter, room temperature

CREAM CHEESE GLAZE

Prepare 1 batch (page 240)

Tip

If you're looking for a warm place to let your dough rise, try the top of the fridge. The top is usually quite warm from the coils. Alternatively, the top of an oven (not inside) set to 250°F is another great warm spot.

1. To make the bread, in a large bowl, whisk together 2 cups of the flour, the sugar, yeast and salt.

2. Melt the butter in a small saucepan. Remove from the heat and stir in the milk, water and vanilla. Pour the butter mixture over the flour mixture and mix with a spatula until combined.

3. Whisk the eggs in a small bowl, then add to the dough, mixing until the eggs are fully incorporated. Add the remaining ¾ cup + 1 tablespoon of flour and mix until combined.

4. Turn the dough out onto a floured work surface. Knead the dough for 10 minutes or until smooth and elastic. Shape it into a ball and place it in a lightly greased bowl. Cover the bowl with plastic wrap and let sit in a warm place until the dough has doubled in size, about 1 hour.

5. To make the cinnamon sugar filling, combine the brown sugar and cinnamon in a small bowl.

6. Grease a 9- × 5-inch loaf pan with butter or non-stick cooking spray. Punch down the dough and turn it out onto a floured work surface. Knead the dough for a couple of minutes, adding a touch of flour if it is sticky. Pat it into a rectangle approximately 12 × 20 inches. Spread a generous amount of the soft butter all over the dough. Sprinkle the cinnamon sugar evenly over the entire buttered surface. Use a pizza cutter or sharp knife to cleanly cut the dough into 6 strips 2 inches wide and 20 inches long. Gently stack the strips on top of each other. Cut across the pile to create 6 equal stacks.

7. With the cinnamon side facing inward, stand 2 rectangles upright in the pan, touching one side of the pan. (The dough rectangles will not fill the width of the pan.) Place another 2 rectangles so they touch the other side of the pan. Continue to alternate the rectangles, making sure the cinnamon sides face the same direction, except for the last rectangle, which should face inward. Cover with a tea towel and let sit in a warm place to rise until doubled, about 45 minutes.

8. Meanwhile, preheat the oven to 350°F. Bake for 30 minutes or until the top of the bread is dark golden brown. For even baking, rotate the pan front to back halfway through. Allow the bread to cool slightly in the pan.

9. Spoon the cream cheese glaze over the top of the warm loaf. The loaf can be covered and stored in the fridge for up to 3 days.

HOLIDAY GINGERBREAD BUNDT

There are certain flavours we associate with the holidays, and gingerbread is one of them. The combination of ginger and honey in this recipe is comforting and packs lots of flavour, and because it's a Bundt, it doesn't require as much icing as a typical layer cake. It will stay fresh for up to week, so it is a perfect cake to have on hand at the holidays for serving at breakfast or to guests, with tea. Here we top it with a cream cheese glaze, but it pairs equally well with a dollop of whipped cream or our favourite, a scoop of dulce de leche ice cream.

GINGERBREAD BUNDT

2¼ cups all-purpose flour

1½ teaspoons baking soda

1½ teaspoons ground ginger

1½ teaspoons cinnamon

½ teaspoon nutmeg

½ teaspoon ground cloves

1 cup unsalted butter, melted

¾ cup honey

1 large egg, room temperature

1 cup granulated sugar

½ cup water

¼ cup sour cream

CREAM CHEESE GLAZE

Prepare 1 batch (page 240)

Tip

Given the depth of a Bundt pan, it is easier and more accurate to check doneness with a bamboo skewer that is long enough to reach well into the batter. It is always the centre we are checking to gauge doneness.

1. Preheat the oven to 350°F. Grease an 8-inch Bundt pan with butter or non-stick cooking spray.

2. In a medium bowl, whisk together the flour, baking soda, ginger, cinnamon, nutmeg and cloves. In a separate bowl, stir together the melted butter and honey.

3. In the bowl of a stand mixer fitted with the paddle attachment, beat together the egg and sugar on medium speed until light and fluffy, about 4 minutes. With the mixer on medium-low speed, alternate adding the flour mixture in 3 additions and the honey mixture in 2 additions, beginning and ending with the flour mixture. Blend after each addition until combined. Remove the bowl from the mixer and fold in the water and sour cream with a large rubber spatula. Pour the batter into the prepared pan and smooth the top.

4. Bake for 30 to 40 minutes or until a wooden skewer inserted into the centre comes out clean. For even baking, rotate the pan front to back halfway through. Allow the Bundt to cool completely in the pan.

5. Invert the pan over a serving plate and tap the bottom to dislodge the cake. Apply the cream cheese glaze around the top of the Bundt, allowing it to fall over the sides. The Bundt cake can be stored in an airtight container in the fridge for up to 1 week.

CARAMELIZED ALMOND TORTE

Almonds have a longstanding history in baking. Our favourite by far is the Swedish Toscakaka. We thank the brilliant Swede who had the idea to bake what is essentially a gigantic piece of crispy, chewy caramelized almond brittle on top of a cake. Our spin on it is to make the cake with almonds, and the result is a wonderful nutty flavour with a salty-sweet finish from the caramelized nuts.

TORTE

½ cup all-purpose flour

1 teaspoon baking powder

⅛ teaspoon salt

¾ cup raw almonds

¼ cup + ⅓ cup granulated sugar, divided

½ cup unsalted butter, room temperature

4 teaspoons pure vanilla extract

¼ teaspoon almond extract

3 large eggs, room temperature

ALMOND TOPPING

1 cup sliced almonds

¼ cup unsalted butter

¼ cup loosely packed brown sugar

½ teaspoon fleur de sel

4½ teaspoons whole milk

Tip

This cake is best eaten the day it is made, as the caramel topping softens over time.

1. Preheat the oven to 350°F. Grease an 8-inch springform pan with butter or non-stick cooking spray.

2. To make the torte, in a small bowl, whisk together the flour, baking powder and salt; set aside. Combine the almonds and the ¼ cup sugar in a food processor and grind until a fine blend. Do not overmix or a nut paste will form.

3. In the bowl of a stand mixer fitted with the paddle attachment, combine the butter, vanilla, almond extract and the ⅓ cup sugar. Beat on medium speed until light and fluffy, about 3 minutes. Add the eggs one at a time, beating well after each addition, stopping to scrape down the sides of the bowl after each addition.

4. Add the ground almond mixture and mix until just combined. Remove the bowl from the mixer and gently fold in the flour mixture by hand. Spoon the batter into the prepared pan and smooth the top with the back of a spoon or an offset spatula.

5. Bake for 45 to 50 minutes or until a toothpick inserted in the centre comes out clean. For even baking, rotate the pan front to back halfway through. Allow the torte to cool completely in the pan on a wire rack. Do not loosen the sides of the pan.

6. Once the torte has cooled, put an oven rack one level above the middle and preheat the oven to 425°F.

7. Meanwhile, prepare the almond topping. In a small saucepan, combine the almonds, butter, brown sugar, fleur de sel and milk. Stir continuously over medium heat for 5 to 7 minutes, until the sugar has dissolved and the mixture is golden and has the consistency of a thick caramel sauce. Immediately spoon the topping over the almond cake. Spread the topping evenly out to the sides of the pan.

8. Return the torte to the oven and bake for 10 minutes, checking it frequently after the first 5 minutes to make sure the top doesn't get any burnt pieces. It is done when the almond topping is a dark golden colour and looks caramelized like a piece of toffee.

9. Allow the torte to cool completely on a wire rack before removing the sides of the pan. Use a sharp knife to cut into wedges. The torte can be stored in an airtight container at room temperature for up to 2 days. Do not refrigerate it, as that would soften the caramelized top.

FLOURLESS CHOCOLATE TORTE

Flourless chocolate torte is an impressive yet incredibly simple cake to make. It is made with only butter, eggs, chocolate and sugar. Given its simplicity, the quality of the chocolate is of the utmost importance. We recommend using Lindt or Callebaut chocolate, which have excellent mouth feel and flavour. Another great brand is Valrhona, but it might be a bit harder to find. If you love this recipe, play around with different chocolate brands. You will be surprised by how the overall flavour changes.

1⅓ cups coarsely chopped 70% to 85% dark chocolate (8 ounces)

1 cup unsalted butter

6 large eggs, separated, room temperature

1 cup granulated sugar

Tip

You know your egg mixture has reached the ribbon stage when you lift the whisk and the mixture drops back into the bowl in long ribbons.

1. Preheat the oven to 350°F. Grease a 9-inch springform pan with butter or non-stick cooking spray and dust with cocoa powder.

2. In a medium saucepan, bring an inch or so of water to a simmer.

3. Combine the chocolate and butter in a large heatproof bowl and place over the simmering water. Stir until melted and smooth. Remove the bowl from the pot and allow to cool to room temperature.

4. In the bowl of a stand mixer fitted with the whisk attachment, whisk the egg yolks with ½ cup of the sugar on medium speed until they reach the ribbon stage. Transfer to a medium bowl.

5. Thoroughly clean and dry the mixer bowl and the whisk attachment, then place both back on the mixer. Add the egg whites to the bowl and whisk on medium-high speed while adding the remaining ½ cup of sugar in a very slow, steady stream. Continue whisking until soft peaks form.

6. Add the egg yolk mixture and half of the egg whites to the room-temperature chocolate mixture and gently fold until smooth and combined. Do not overmix the batter or it will deflate. Gently but thoroughly fold in the remaining egg whites. Spoon the batter into prepared pan.

7. Bake for 30 minutes or until a toothpick inserted in the centre comes out clean. (This batter is very fragile, so do not rotate the pan during baking.) Allow the torte to cool completely in the pan on a wire rack. Once cooled, gently remove the sides of the pan. The torte can be stored in an airtight container at room temperature for up to 3 days.

Recipe is naturally gluten-free.

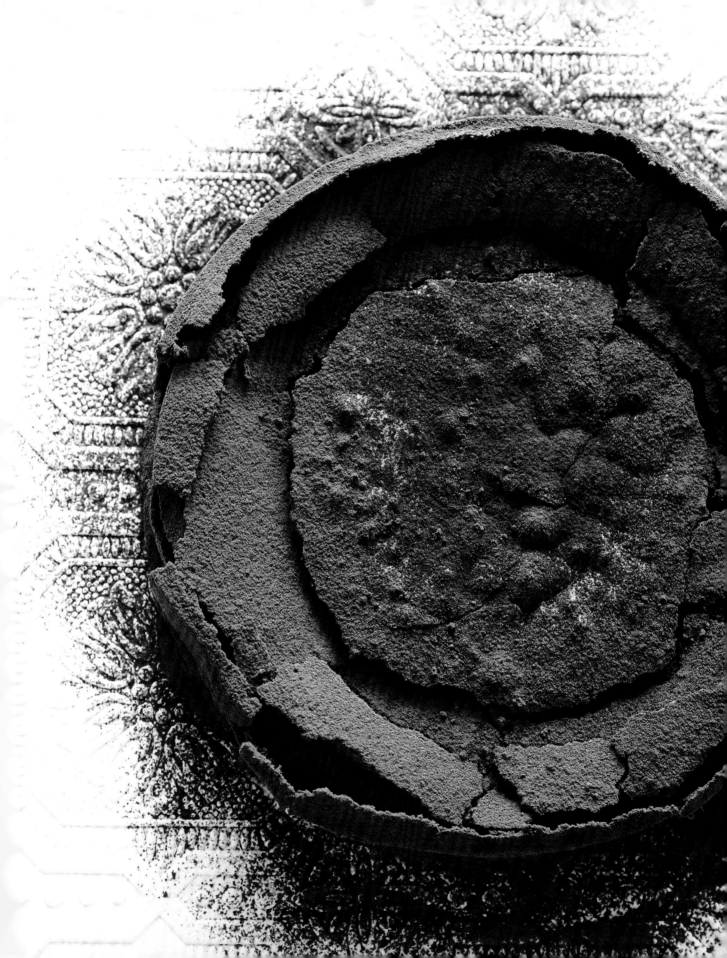

Quick and Easy
SUMMER FRUIT TORTE

At Bobbette & Belle we are known for making decadent layer cakes, but a simple fruit torte is a quick and easy cake that is perfect served as dessert with some vanilla ice cream or for breakfast with coffee. People often feel intimidated making dessert for a professional baker, but let us be the first to say that there is nothing we love more than having somebody else make dessert. We're in pastry because we have a genuine passion for sweets, and that means the more variety, the better. This dessert stems from an apple torte that our good friend Liz makes. We both fell in love with it the first time we tried it. We make our version with stone fruits and berries, but it is so versatile you could use almost any fruit and it would be a success. We regard this as a staple recipe in that it is quick and easy but also allows for flexibility and creativity.

3 cups sliced assorted stone fruits (peaches, nectarines, apricots, plums)

1 cup assorted berries (such as raspberries, blueberries and blackberries)

1½ cups all-purpose flour

1½ teaspoons baking powder

⅛ teaspoon cinnamon

⅛ teaspoon nutmeg

⅛ teaspoon salt

½ cup whole milk

¼ cup sour cream

½ cup unsalted butter, room temperature

1 cup granulated sugar

2 large eggs

1 teaspoon pure vanilla extract

Tip

You can use many types of fruits, depending on what is in season. We love making an apple version in the fall and winter. We recommend sticking to fresh fruit, as frozen fruit will be too wet in this torte. It is also wonderful served warm with a little ice cream or Crème Anglaise (page 244).

1. Preheat the oven to 350°F. Grease a 9-inch springform pan with butter or non-stick cooking spray. Lightly flour the pan, tapping out any excess. To make the springform pan watertight, wrap the outside in tin foil.

2. Wash the fruit and berries. Remove the pits from the stone fruits and slice ½-inch thick. Lay out your slices of fruit and the berries on paper towels to absorb any extra liquid and set aside while you prepare the batter.

3. In a small bowl, whisk together the flour, baking powder, cinnamon, nutmeg and salt. In another small bowl, stir together the milk and sour cream.

4. In the bowl of a stand mixer fitted with the paddle attachment, cream the butter and sugar on medium speed until light and fluffy, about 3 minutes. Beat in the eggs one at a time, beating well after each addition and stopping once to scrape down the sides of the bowl. Add the vanilla and beat to combine.

5. With the mixer on low speed, alternately add the flour mixture in 3 additions and the milk mixture in 2 additions, beginning and ending with the flour mixture. Blend just until combined, taking care not to overmix the batter. Pour the batter into the prepared pan. Lay the fruit slices in a single layer on top of the batter, leaving the berries on the paper towel for now.

6. Bake for 45 minutes, then quickly remove from the oven and top with the berries, lightly pressing the berries into the top of the cake. Return to the oven to bake for an additional 15 minutes, until the batter that has risen to the top is golden brown and a toothpick inserted in the batter comes out clean. Allow the torte to cool in the pan for 10 minutes before removing the sides of the pan. Cool completely on a wire rack. The torte can be stored, wrapped in plastic wrap and then tin foil, in the fridge for up to 3 days.

5

CRUMBLES TARTS AND PIES

APPLE CRUMBLE

Certain recipes commit themselves to memory, and apple crumble is one of them. Once you have made it a few times you will be able to whip it up easily, even without the recipe. It is simple to make and quite forgiving if some of the ratios are slightly off. There is an intuitive element to savoury cooking that is difficult to replicate in pastry making. So much of what we do is based on science and exact measurements, so it is rare that you are able to tweak as you go along, but this is a recipe that allows you to do that. We love the idea of offering recipes that may well become a part of your roster of go-to desserts.

APPLE FILLING

14 Granny Smith or other firm, tart apples, peeled, cored and sliced ¼ inch thick

1 tablespoon lemon juice

1½ cups granulated sugar

½ cup all-purpose flour

1¾ teaspoons cinnamon

¾ teaspoon salt

½ cup unsalted butter

CRUMBLE TOPPING

2½ cups all-purpose flour

2¼ cups pecans, coarsely chopped

2 cups large-flake rolled oats

1 cup + 2 tablespoons loosely packed brown sugar

1½ teaspoons cinnamon

¼ teaspoon salt

1½ cups cold unsalted butter, cut into 1-inch cubes

1. Preheat the oven to 350°F. Lightly grease a 9- × 13-inch baking pan with butter or non-stick cooking spray.

2. To make the apple filling, in a large bowl, toss the apple slices with the lemon juice. In small bowl, whisk together the sugar, flour, cinnamon and salt. Add to the apples and toss to evenly coat.

3. In a large skillet, melt the butter over medium heat. Add the apple mixture, reduce the heat to low and cook the apples, uncovered and stirring occasionally, until they are tender and the sauce thickens, 8 to 10 minutes. Spread the apples in an even layer in the prepared baking dish.

4. To make the crumble topping, in a large bowl combine the flour, pecans, oats, brown sugar, cinnamon and salt. Add the butter and work it in with your fingers until the mixture begins to stick together in clumps and the butter pieces resemble coarse meal. Sprinkle the crumble evenly over the apples.

5. Bake for 30 to 40 minutes or until the filling starts to bubble and the topping is golden brown. For even baking, rotate the pan front to back halfway through. Allow the crumble to cool slightly before serving. The crumble can be covered and stored in the fridge for up to 4 days.

 Tip We love a nice thick, chunky crumble as opposed to a sandy one, so you need to work the topping enough to form clumps, but don't overwork it or it will turn into a ball of dough.

MIXED BERRY TART
with Vanilla Pastry Cream

Some version of this tart has been, without a doubt, on almost every dessert and pastry shop menu at one point or another, and as with most popular things, its ubiquity has led to some unfortunate bastardization. It makes us cringe, but it also makes us want to sing the praises of the real deal. Few desserts are more pleasing than a buttery, sweet crust filled with impossibly silky vanilla pastry cream and topped with fresh seasonal fruit.

PÂTE SUCRÉE (SWEET PASTRY)

½ cup + 1 tablespoon unsalted butter, room temperature

½ cup granulated sugar

⅛ teaspoon salt

1 large egg

1¾ cups all-purpose flour

VANILLA PASTRY CREAM

Prepare 1 batch (page 243)

MIXED BERRY TOPPING

½ pint fresh raspberries

½ pint fresh blueberries

½ pint fresh blackberries

½ pint fresh strawberries, hulled

Tip

Chilling your tart shell before baking helps prevent shrinkage.

This dough can be made in advance and frozen for up to 1 month.

1. To make the sweet pastry dough, in the bowl of a stand mixer fitted with the paddle attachment, cream the butter, sugar and salt on medium speed until light and fluffy, about 3 minutes. Beat in the egg until well combined. Stop the mixer and scrape down the sides of the bowl.

2. With the mixer on medium-low speed, slowly add the flour, mixing just until incorporated and the dough just comes together. Flatten the dough into a disc, wrap it in plastic wrap and chill it in the fridge for at least 2 hours.

3. Preheat the oven to 350°F. Have ready either a 14- × 4½-inch rectangular tart pan with removable bottom or an 8-inch round tart pan with removable bottom. It is not necessary to grease your tart pan.

4. On a lightly floured surface, roll the dough out to a ⅛-inch thick rectangle or circle that is 2 inches larger than your tart pan. (If the dough cracks, let it rest for a few minutes to warm up slightly before continuing to roll.) Roll the dough around the rolling pin and then unroll it over the tart pan. Gently press the dough into the sides, corners and bottom of the pan. To ensure a clean edge, use a knife to cut off the excess dough. Prick the entire bottom of the crust with a fork, being very careful to score the top but not fully pierce through to the bottom. Chill in the freezer for 15 minutes or until firm to the touch.

5. To blind bake the tart shell, line it with a large piece of parchment paper, then fill it with about 2 cups of dried beans. Bake for 12 to 15 minutes, until a light golden colour. Remove the parchment paper and the beans, rotate the tart shell to ensure even baking and continue to bake for another 10 minutes or until lightly golden in colour. Allow the tart shell to cool completely in the pan on a wire rack.

6. Unmould the cooled tart shell and place it on a serving platter. Spoon the pastry cream into the tart shell. Use a small offset spatula to smooth out the pastry cream.

7. Wash and dry all the berries, and cut the strawberries into halves or into quarters if large. Arrange the berries on top of the pastry cream to fully cover the top of the tart. Serve immediately or keep in the fridge until served. The finished tart can be stored, covered, in the fridge for up to 2 days.

APPLE GALETTES

Luisa, a good friend of ours, served apple galettes for dessert at her wedding in Napa Valley. Such a simple dessert, but one that left everybody talking and secretly hoping for seconds. Two wonderful things about a galette: the ratio of fruit filling to crust feels both decadent and comforting, and it's so easy to prepare.

GALETTE PASTRY

1⅔ cups all-purpose flour

3 tablespoons granulated sugar

¼ teaspoon salt

¾ cup + 2 tablespoons cold unsalted butter, cut into 1-inch cubes

¼ cup ice water

APPLE FILLING

4 Granny Smith or other firm apples, peeled, cored and sliced ¼ inch thick

Juice of ½ lemon

¼ cup loosely packed brown sugar

2 tablespoons all-purpose flour

½ teaspoon cinnamon

¼ teaspoon salt

2 teaspoons unsalted butter

½ cup water

¼ cup chopped pecans

EGG WASH

1 large egg

1 tablespoon water

Tip

The galettes may be prepared (but not baked) ahead of time and frozen. Brush the frozen galettes with the egg wash before baking and increase the baking time by 10 minutes.

1. To make the galette pastry, in a medium bowl, whisk together the flour, sugar and salt. Cut in the butter with a pastry cutter until most of the butter is pea sized. Break up any larger pieces by pressing them between your fingers to form thin slivers of butter. Drizzle over the water and stir gently with a large spoon until the dough just starts to stick together. Turn the dough out onto a work surface and form a disc by pushing it together a few times. Do not knead the dough.

2. Lightly flour your work surface and roll out the dough to a 9- × 11-inch rectangle. Fold the dough in thirds, like folding a business letter. Rotate the dough 90 degrees, roll it out a second time to a 9- × 11-inch rectangle and once again fold the dough in thirds. Wrap the dough in plastic wrap and refrigerate for 2 hours.

3. Line 2 baking sheets with parchment paper. On a lightly floured work surface, roll out the dough to ⅛-inch thickness. Using a 6-inch round cutter, or using a 6-inch plate as a guide, cut out 5 rounds. Lay the rounds on the lined baking sheets and place in the fridge to chill while you make the apple filling.

4. To make the apple filling, in a large bowl, toss the apple slices with the lemon juice. In a small bowl, whisk together the sugar, flour, cinnamon and salt.

5. In a large skillet over medium heat, melt the butter and the sugar mixture in the water. Add the apples and cook, stirring occasionally, for 5 minutes or until they have softened slightly. Do not overcook the apples or they will become mushy. Remove from the heat and allow to cool to room temperature.

6. Put oven racks in the upper and lower thirds of the oven. Preheat the oven to 350°F.

7. Take the pastry rounds out of the fridge and spoon the cooled apple filling evenly onto the centre of each round. Let sit until the dough is workable, then carefully fold the edges of the pastry up over the apples, but do not completely cover the filling. Pinch the edges of the pastry together to ensure it stays folded over the apples. Evenly sprinkle the pecans over the filling.

8. In a small bowl, beat together the egg and water with a fork, then lightly brush the pastry with the egg wash.

9. Bake for 25 to 30 minutes or until the pastry is golden brown. For even baking, rotate the baking sheets front to back and top to bottom halfway through. Allow the galettes to cool slightly before serving.

SKILLET PEACH COBBLER

Certain recipes were created to take advantage of seasonal fruit crops and highlight their strengths. They are quick to execute and often use basic ingredients found in most pantries. Cobblers are a great example of this type of recipe. Here in Ontario we are in the middle of peach season as we write our book, and peach cobbler perfectly illustrates how simple ingredients and cooking methods can highlight and enhance a fruit's natural flavour. In fact, peaches are often synonymous with cobbler because they have a lot of natural juice and quickly caramelize with heat. The biscuit top balances out the sweetness and absorbs some of the natural juice. We love the idea of baking cobbler right in the skillet, but it is just as easily baked in ramekins or a single large baking dish.

PEACH FILLING

8 ripe peaches, peeled, pitted and sliced into wedges

1 tablespoon lemon juice

⅓ cup unsalted butter

1 cup loosely packed brown sugar

2 tablespoons bourbon

1 teaspoon pure vanilla extract

BISCUIT TOPPING

2¾ cups all-purpose flour

1 cup granulated sugar

2 tablespoons + ½ teaspoon baking powder

½ teaspoon salt

¾ cup cold unsalted butter, cut into 1-inch cubes

½ cup buttermilk

1 large egg

1 large egg yolk

EGG WASH

1 large egg

1 tablespoon water

1. Preheat the oven to 350°F. The ramekins do not need to be greased.

2. To make the peach filling, in a large bowl toss the peaches with the lemon juice.

3. In a large skillet over medium-high heat, melt the butter with the brown sugar. Add the peaches and bring to a boil, stirring occasionally until the syrup thickens, about 5 minutes. Remove from the heat and stir in the bourbon and vanilla. Allow the filling to cool completely.

4. To make the biscuit topping, combine the flour, sugar, baking powder, salt and butter in the bowl of a stand mixer fitted with the paddle attachment. Mix on medium-low speed just until the butter is pea sized.

5. In a separate bowl, whisk together the buttermilk, egg and egg yolk. With the mixer on low speed, add the buttermilk mixture to the flour mixture, mixing only until the dough comes together. Do not overmix.

6. Divide the cooled peach filling evenly among the ramekins. Top each ramekin with 4 heaping tablespoons of the biscuit topping.

7. In a small bowl, beat together the egg and water with a fork, then lightly brush the biscuit topping with the egg wash.

8. Arrange the ramekins on a baking sheet and bake for 30 minutes or until the tops are golden brown and filling is bubbling. For even baking, rotate the baking sheet front to back halfway through. Allow the cobblers to cool slightly before servings. The cobblers can be covered and refrigerated for up to 3 days.

Tip Warm cobbler is wonderful with vanilla ice cream, but we love to serve it with Crème Anglaise (page 244), which adds a touch of creaminess without overpowering the dessert or making it seem heavy.

SALTED CARAMEL TART
with Dark Chocolate Glaze

What could be better than taking a nice light, buttery tart crust and filling it with thick, golden salted caramel and topping it off with rich dark chocolate? It's so decadent, it's almost absurd. The key is the caramel filling. Getting the timing right ensures that it will have a pronounced caramel flavour while being soft but not too runny. Leonardo da Vinci once said that "simplicity is the ultimate sophistication," and that sums up this recipe perfectly.

PÂTE SUCRÉE (SWEET PASTRY)

Prepare and blind bake 1 batch (steps 1 through 5, page 132)

SALTED CARAMEL FILLING

2 cups granulated sugar

½ cup water

¼ cup corn syrup

½ cup unsalted butter, cut into chunks, room temperature

½ cup 35% cream

2 tablespoons sour cream

¾ teaspoon fleur de sel, plus more for garnish

CHOCOLATE GLAZE AND GARNISH

Prepare ½ batch of Chocolate Glaze (page 239)

Fleur de sel or pink Himalayan salt, to taste

Tip

We are huge fans of fleur de sel, but for the photo we opted to garnish with pink Himalayan salt to add a touch of soft blush colour to the smooth dark chocolate glaze.

1. To make the caramel filling, in a saucepan over medium-high heat, bring the sugar, water and corn syrup to a boil, then boil, swirling the pan occasionally to prevent burning, until the caramel becomes a golden colour, about 7 minutes. Carefully (the mixture will bubble up) add the butter, 35% cream, sour cream and fleur de sel, then whisk until the caramel is smooth. Immediately pour the caramel filling into the baked tart shell. Chill in the fridge for at least 4 hours.

2. Pour the chocolate glaze over the set caramel filling. It should be flush with the top of the crust. Carefully place the tart back in the fridge to set up for 30 minutes.

3. Garnish the tart before serving by sprinkling a thin line of fleur de sel down the centre of the glazed tart. The finished tart can be stored, covered, in the fridge for up to 3 days—any longer, the chocolate glaze will dry out and start to crack.

CLASSIC CANADIAN BUTTER TARTS

There are some desserts—hello, butter tarts—that are uniquely Canadian, and as such we feel quite strongly about what constitutes a winning version. For us, a butter tart should have a buttery, almost salty crust and the filling should be cooked but still give way to a slightly runny centre. Perhaps a better word is "oozing"—the filling should look like lava. In many savoury kitchens the mark of a good chef is the ability to cook an egg properly. For us, it's the ability to bake a butter tart well.

PÂTE BRISÉE (PIE PASTRY)

1¼ cups all-purpose flour

2 teaspoons granulated sugar

1 teaspoon salt

½ cup cold unsalted butter

1 large egg

2 teaspoons cold water

FILLING

3 large eggs

½ teaspoon pure vanilla extract

Rounded ¼ teaspoon salt

1 cup loosely packed brown sugar

⅓ cup unsalted butter

4 tablespoons + 1½ teaspoons honey

4 tablespoons + 1½ teaspoons corn syrup

2 tablespoons + 2 teaspoons 35% cream

¾ teaspoon vinegar

Tip

This dough can be made in advance and frozen for up to 1 month.

1. To make the pastry, in a medium bowl whisk together the flour, sugar and salt. Using the large holes of a box grater, grate the cold butter over the flour mixture. Gently blend the butter into the flour with your fingers until it resembles a coarse meal. Take cake not to overmix the butter at this point.

2. In a small bowl, whisk together the egg and cold water. Drizzle over the flour in 3 additions, gently mixing with a large spoon until the wet ingredients are absorbed and the dough just comes together.

3. Turn the dough out onto a work surface and press it together with your hands until it forms a ball. Flatten the dough into a disc, wrap it in plastic wrap and chill it in the fridge for at least 3 hours.

4. Preheat the oven to 350°F. Have ready a 12-cup muffin pan. The muffin cups do not need to be greased.

5. On a lightly floured work surface, roll the dough out to ⅛-inch thickness. Using a 4-inch round cookie cutter, cut out 12 rounds. Delicately press each round into the bottom and sides of the muffin cups, making small overlapping pleats to fit the dough into the sides properly. Make sure the pastry extends ½-inch above the edge of the muffin cups to allow for shrinkage. Place the pan in the freezer for 15 minutes or until the dough is firm to the touch.

6. To blind bake the tart shells, line them with paper muffin liners that have been half filled with dried beans. Bake for 15 minutes or until the edges are lightly browned. Remove the liners and beans, rotate the pan front to back to ensure even baking and continue to bake for another 8 to 10 minutes or until the shells are a light golden colour. Allow the tart shells to cool completely in the pan on a wire rack. Once cool, knock the baked shells out of the muffin pan and arrange on a parchment-lined baking sheet.

7. Preheat the oven to 325°F.

8. To make the filling, in a large bowl whisk together the eggs, vanilla, salt and half the brown sugar until smooth. Set aside.

9. In a large saucepan, melt the butter over medium heat. Once the butter has melted, whisk in the other half of the brown sugar, the honey, corn syrup and cream. Continue to heat, whisking constantly until the brown sugar has dissolved. Remove from the heat.

10. Pour a small amount of the hot sugar mixture into the egg mixture, whisking constantly. Continue adding the hot sugar mixture a little at a time, whisking constantly, then whisk in the vinegar.

11. Strain the filling through a fine-mesh sieve into a bowl, then divide the filling between the tart shells. The filling should be flush with the top of the tarts.

12. Bake for 16 to 18 minutes or until the filling still has a slight jiggle. For even baking, rotate the baking sheet front to back halfway through. Transfer the butter tarts to a wire rack and allow to cool completely. The butter tarts can be stored in an airtight container in the fridge for up to 1 week.

MILE-HIGH LEMON MERINGUE PIE

Most people love a good lemon meringue pie. The combination of tart and sweet is almost universally pleasing, so it has always seemed strange to us that so few people know how to make it. It's true that preparing lemon curd can seem a little daunting, but it is actually a very simple recipe to master once you know a few easy tips. Free of thickeners, preservatives and artificial flavours, fresh lemon curd, like we make at the shop, is naturally thickened by cooking the eggs. In addition, we add butter, which gives the curd an extremely silky and smooth texture.

PÂTE SUCRÉE (SWEET PASTRY)

Prepare and blind bake 1 batch (steps 1 through 5, page 132)

LEMON CURD

1 cup granulated sugar

4 large eggs

2 large egg yolks

½ cup fresh lemon juice, strained

⅔ cup unsalted butter, cut into 1-inch pieces, room temperature

MERINGUE TOPPING

4 large egg whites

½ cup granulated sugar

⅛ teaspoon cream of tartar

Tip

When making the lemon curd, do not let your eggs, yolks and sugar sit together unwhisked, otherwise the sugar will "cook" the eggs.

1. Preheat the oven to 325°F.

2. To make the lemon curd, in a medium saucepan, heat an inch or so of water until barely simmering. In a large heatproof bowl, whisk together the sugar, eggs and egg yolks until well combined. Slowly pour in the lemon juice, whisking constantly.

3. Place the bowl over the barely simmering water to create your own double boiler. Do not let the bowl touch the simmering water or the eggs will scramble. Whisking constantly, cook until the curd thickens to the ribbon stage (when the whisk is lifted from the bowl, the curd falls back into the bowl like a falling ribbon), about 10 minutes. Remove the bowl from the pot (set the pot aside—you'll need it later) and whisk in the butter pieces one at a time, whisking until each piece is fully incorporated before adding the next. Then, using a rubber spatula, press the curd through a fine-mesh sieve into a clean bowl, making sure to scrape the underside of the sieve to get all the curd.

4. Pour the lemon curd into the baked tart shell. Bake for 25 minutes or until the curd is set. It should jiggle slightly but not look runny. Allow the tart to cool completely on a rack before placing it in the fridge to chill for 3 or 4 hours.

5. To make the meringue topping, return the pot of water to a bare simmer. In the clean, dry bowl of a stand mixer, whisk together the egg whites and sugar. Place the bowl over the barely simmering water and continue whisking until the mixture is warm and the sugar has dissolved. Remove the bowl from the pot and add the cream of tartar.

6. Place the bowl on the mixer and fit it with the whisk attachment. Whisk the egg whites on medium speed until the meringue is cool to the touch, tripled in volume and holds stiff peaks.

7. Put an oven rack in the upper third of the oven and preheat the broiler. Heap the meringue on top of the chilled tart in peaks making sure to spread it right to the edge. Use the back of the spoon to shape peaks and swirls in the meringue. Broil until the meringue peaks are golden, about 3 minutes. Serve immediately or keep in the fridge until served. The finished pie can be covered and stored in the fridge for up to 2 days.

COCONUT BANANA CREAM PIE

In baking, textural differences are generally regarded as one of the characteristics of a successful recipe, but in this case, we're convinced that it is the barely discernible layer upon layer of soft, silky banana, custard and cream that leads to knee-weakening satisfaction. We love to take a great classic dessert and bring it to the next level. In this case, rather than the usual layered bananas, we have cooked some of them down with caramel to create a layer of caramelized banana "jam," which we then top with sliced bananas, a light coconut custard and of course copious amounts of whipped cream.

PÂTE BRISÉE (PIE PASTRY)

Prepare—but do not blind bake—1 batch (steps 1 through 3, page 140)

CARAMELIZED BANANA JAM

1½ ripe bananas

¼ cup loosely packed brown sugar

1 tablespoon water

2 teaspoons fresh lemon juice

⅛ teaspoon fleur de sel

1 teaspoon pure vanilla extract

COCONUT PASTRY CREAM

Prepare 1 batch of Vanilla Pastry Cream (page 243)

⅓ cup shredded coconut, toasted (page 12)

1 ripe banana

CHANTILLY CREAM

1½ cups 35% cream

4½ teaspoons icing sugar

1 teaspoon pure vanilla extract

2 tablespoons shredded coconut, for garnish

1. Preheat the oven to 350°F. Have ready an ungreased, 9-inch pie dish.

2. On a lightly floured work surface, roll the pastry dough out to an 11-inch circle that is ⅛-inch thick. Roll the dough around the rolling pin and then unroll it over the pie dish. Gently press the dough lightly into the sides and bottom of the dish, leaving a 1-inch overhang of dough. Crimp the dough between your fingers to create a rustic, slightly ruffled edge to the pie crust. Prick the entire bottom of the crust with a fork, being very careful to score the top but not fully pierce through to the bottom. Chill the pie shell in the freezer for 15 minutes or until firm to the touch.

3. To blind bake the pie shell, line it with a large piece of parchment paper, then fill it with about 3 cups of dried beans. Bake for 15 minutes or until the edges are golden. Remove the parchment paper and beans, rotate the pie shell to ensure even baking and continue to bake for another 10 minutes or until lightly golden all over. Allow the pie shell to cool completely on a wire rack.

4. To make the caramelized banana jam, mash the bananas in a bowl and set aside. In a small pot over medium-high heat, bring the brown sugar, water, lemon juice and fleur de sel to a boil. Reduce the heat and add the bananas, then simmer for 5 minutes, constantly stirring until thick and jammy. Remove from the heat and stir in the vanilla. Cover and leave the banana jam to cool completely.

5. To make the coconut pastry cream, blitz the toasted coconut in a food processor until it resembles fine crumbs. Gently fold the coconut into the vanilla pastry cream.

6. To assemble the pie, spread the banana jam in the bottom of the pie shell. Cut the ripe banana into thin slices and arrange in a single layer over the banana jam. Spread the coconut pastry cream on top of the bananas. Cover the filled pie with plastic wrap and place in the fridge to set for 6 to 8 hours.

7. When ready to serve, make the Chantilly cream: Whip the cream, icing sugar and vanilla to medium peaks. Spread the cream over the pie and out to the edges. Garnish with coconut and serve. Leftovers can be stored in an airtight container in the fridge for up to 2 days.

MINI BLUEBERRY HAND PIES

Blueberry pie holds a firm place next to apple and lemon as one of the most popular North American pies. However, it is perhaps not enjoyed as often as it could be because it doesn't store or transport well beyond the first day. The berries continue to release juice, softening the pie and making for messy leftovers. Enter hand pies, which are, for all intents and purposes, "pop tarts" for foodies. We have reduced the blueberry filling longer than is typical for a pie in order to create a more stable filling. The greater ratio of crust to filling ensures easy portability, and using a sweet dough crust, which holds its shape, allows for lots of creativity.

BLUEBERRY FILLING

1 tablespoon cornstarch

2 tablespoons water

½ teaspoon pure vanilla extract

1 cup frozen blueberries

3 tablespoons granulated sugar

1 tablespoon fresh lemon juice

⅛ teaspoon salt

PÂTE SUCRÉE (SWEET PASTRY)

Prepare—but do not blind bake—1 batch (steps 1 and 2, page 132)

EGG WASH

1 large egg

1 tablespoon water

Tip

If you are feeling daunted by the lattice pattern but still want to be creative, cut 12 rounds for the tops, then use a tiny round, square or diamond-shaped cutter to cut rows of one of the shapes all over each top. The effect will be much like a lattice without all the required weaving.

1. To make the blueberry filling, in a small bowl, stir together the cornstarch, water and vanilla until it forms a paste.

2. In a medium saucepan, stir together the frozen blueberries, sugar, lemon juice and salt. Bring to a boil over medium heat, stirring constantly. Stir the cornstarch mixture again, add it to the blueberries and continue to cook, stirring constantly until the mixture thickens, about 5 minutes. Transfer the filling to a bowl and allow to it cool completely in the fridge before using.

3. Preheat the oven to 350°F. Line a baking sheet with parchment paper. In a small bowl, whisk together the egg and water; set aside the egg wash.

4. On a lightly floured work surface, roll the pastry dough out to ¼-inch thickness. Using a 3-inch round cookie cutter, cut out 24 rounds if you are making a simple top or 12 rounds if you are making a lattice top. You may have to gather the scraps and reroll the dough if you cannot get 24 circles from the first roll. If you have to reroll the dough more than two times, let it rest in the fridge for 30 minutes before rolling out again.

5. Place 1½ teaspoons of the blueberry filling in the centre of 12 rounds.

6. For a simple top, use a ½-inch round cutter to cut out the centre of the other 12 rounds. Lightly brush the egg wash onto the edges of the rounds that have the filling. Place the rounds with the cut-outs over the filling. Using a fork, lightly press down on the edges to seal the tops to the bottoms.

7. Using an offset spatula, transfer the hand pies to the lined baking sheet, arranging them 1-inch apart. Chill in the fridge for 15 minutes before baking.

8. Brush the tops of the pies with the egg wash. Bake for 25 to 30 minutes or until the pastry is golden. For even baking, rotate the baking sheet front to back halfway through. Allow the pies to cool slightly before serving. The finished pies can be stored in an airtight container for up to 4 days.

PERFECT PUMPKIN PIE

Pumpkin pie is traditionally enjoyed during harvest time in North America. Puréed pumpkin is fairly bland in flavour but it has a smooth and creamy texture, which is perfect for desserts. The keys to a great pumpkin pie are a buttery crust and proper seasoning of the filling. The delicate balance and wide variety of the spices in our filling, along with the sour cream and condensed milk, give it a delicious robust flavour and ensure it's worthy of Thanksgiving dinner. Just make sure you use pure pumpkin purée, not pumpkin pie filling.

PÂTE SUCRÉE (SWEET PASTRY)

Prepare and blind bake 1 batch (steps 1 through 5, page 132)

PUMPKIN FILLING

1¼ cups canned pumpkin purée

½ cup sweetened condensed milk

2 tablespoons sour cream

½ teaspoon cinnamon

¼ teaspoon ground ginger

⅛ teaspoon ground allspice

⅛ teaspoon nutmeg

1 large egg

½ teaspoon pure vanilla extract

CHANTILLY CREAM

¾ cup 35% cream

1 tablespoon icing sugar

½ teaspoon pure vanilla extract

1. Preheat the oven to 350°F.

2. To make the pumpkin filling, in a medium bowl whisk together the pumpkin purée, condensed milk, sour cream, cinnamon, ginger, allspice and nutmeg. Add the egg and vanilla and whisk until well combined.

3. Pour the filling into the baked pie shell and bake for 30 minutes or until the filling is just set. If you gently jiggle the tart, the filling should not move. For even baking, rotate the pie front to back halfway through. Allow the tart to cool completely before serving.

4. When ready to serve, make the Chantilly cream: Whip the cream, icing sugar and vanilla until the cream holds medium-stiff peaks. Dollop the Chantilly cream on top of the tart. The finished tart can be covered and stored in the fridge for up to 3 days.

Tip If you want to create a sweet dough garnish that encircles the top of the tart, simply roll out the dough scraps and, using a small leaf cutter, punch out as many small leaves as the extra dough will allow. Brush with egg wash and bake on a parchment-lined cookie sheet at 350°F until golden. Place the cooled leaves all around the outer edge of the tart to create a wreath.

6

FRENCH MACARONS

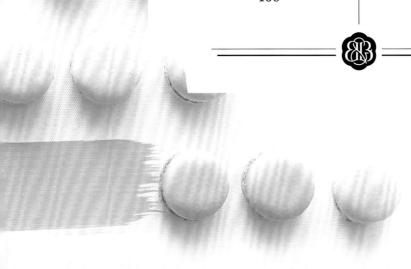

FRENCH MACARON SHELLS

1 cup + 2 tablespoons icing sugar

1⅓ cups almond flour

½ cup granulated sugar

⅛ teaspoon salt

½ cup egg whites (from 4 large eggs), room temperature

Recipe is naturally gluten-free.

Recipe is naturally dairy-free.

Tip

Once the shells are cool, pair them with shells of a similar size to create sandwiches. The shells can be filled immediately or stored in an airtight container in the freezer for up to a month.

1. Put oven racks in the upper and lower thirds of the oven and preheat the oven to 300°F. Line 2 baking sheets with parchment paper (or silicone baking mats if you're experienced with piping macarons and don't need to trace circles). The parchment must lie flat inside the baking sheet, so trim if necessary. Using a 2-inch round cookie cutter as a guide, trace 48 circles, an inch apart, onto the paper with a pencil. Flip over the parchment to prevent pencil marks transferring to your macarons.

2. Sift the icing sugar into a medium bowl, then add the almond flour and whisk to combine. In a small bowl, stir together the granulated sugar and salt.

3. In the bowl of a stand mixer fitted with the whisk attachment, whisk the egg whites on medium speed until frothy. Slowly add the sugar mixture a spoonful at a time while whisking. Increase the speed to medium-high and whip until the meringue is glossy and holds medium peaks. Scrape into a large, wide bowl.

4. Add one-third of the almond mixture and fold together with a large rubber spatula. Fold in the remaining almond mixture in 2 additions, continuing to fold until the batter is completely combined and soft but thick—it should flow back into itself, much like the consistency of running lava. The meringue will deflate, but do not overmix or the finished shells may tilt or lose their lacy foot.

5. Fit a large piping bag with a ½-inch plain round tip (#5 is standard). Fill the piping bag half full so it will be easy to handle. Secure the top with a clip or elastic. Holding the piping bag upright just above the baking sheet and in the middle of your pencilled circle, squeeze out a mound of batter, stopping just before it reaches the edge of the circle. Repeat until the batter is finished. Work quickly when you refill the bag to avoid mixing the batter any further. Once all the shells are piped, gently tap the bottom of each baking sheet against the counter to knock out any air bubbles and to smooth out the tops.

6. Allow the piped shells to sit, uncovered for 30 minutes or until a thin skin forms. (This will assist in creating the much-desired lacy foot.) The shells should feel dry to the touch on top. The length of time they need to sit will vary depending on the time of year and the humidity.

7. Bake for 4 minutes. Rotate the baking sheets front to back and top to bottom and bake for another 4 minutes. Rotate the sheets once more and bake for 6 minutes or until the macarons have a lacy foot and a smooth, crisp, slightly shiny top that is uniform in colour. If you lightly touch the top, it should not deflate or give. If the top seems to slide slightly, bake for 2 more minutes and test again. Allow the shells to cool on the baking sheets.

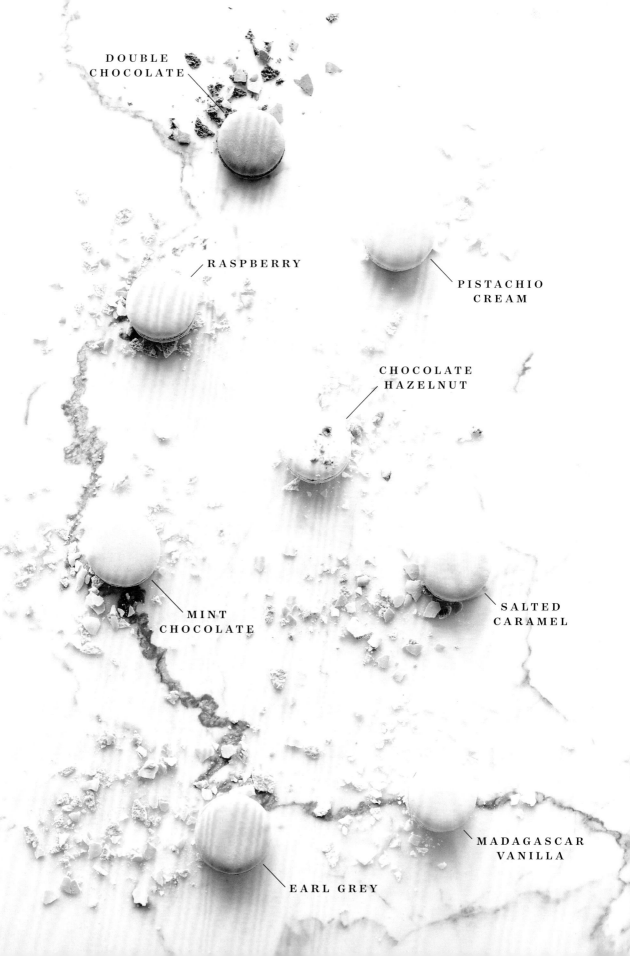

DOUBLE
CHOCOLATE

RASPBERRY

PISTACHIO
CREAM

CHOCOLATE
HAZELNUT

MINT
CHOCOLATE

SALTED
CARAMEL

MADAGASCAR
VANILLA

EARL GREY

CHOCOLATE

Whisk $\frac{1}{4}$ cup cocoa powder into the almond and icing sugar mixture.

If you desire a darker colour than the cocoa provides, when beating the meringue, add 2 drops of brown and 1 drop of black food colouring. We use Americolor gel colours (see source guide, page 248).

HAZELNUT

When beating the meringue, add 2 drops of ivory food colouring. We use Americolor gel colours (see source guide, page 248).

Lightly sprinkle the piped shells with $\frac{1}{3}$ cup toasted and coarsely chopped hazelnuts before setting aside to dry.

MINT CHOCOLATE

When beating the meringue, add 2 drops of sky blue and 1 drop of green food colouring. We use Americolor gel colours (see source guide, page 248).

SALTED CARAMEL

Add $\frac{1}{2}$ teaspoon pure coffee extract to the meringue just before it is finished beating.

Just after adding the coffee extract, add 2 drops of yellow and 5 drops of ivory food colouring. We use Americolor gel colours (see source guide, page 248).

EARL GREY

When beating the meringue, add 8 drops of orange and 1 drop of soft pink food colouring. We use Americolor gel colours (see source guide, page 248).

PISTACHIO

When beating the meringue, add 2 drops of avocado green and 2 drops of electric green food colouring. We use Americolor gel colours (see source guide, page 248).

RASPBERRY

When beating the meringue, add 1 drop of soft pink food colouring. We use Americolor gel colours (see source guide, page 248).

VANILLA

Add 1 teaspoon pure vanilla extract to the meringue just before it is finished beating.

MADAGASCAR VANILLA MACARONS

Fine vanilla is much like fine wine, in that quality and source have a significant bearing on flavour. Vanilla is produced in several tropical climates, but it is Tahitian and Madagascar vanilla that are particularly sought after. The vanilla bean is the fruit of a species of orchid that flowers only once a year and must be hand pollinated to produce the fruit, and the fruit must also be hand picked—all of which helps explain why natural vanilla is one of the most expensive spices in the world. It can be tempting to use an inexpensive artificial vanilla extract in baking, but we encourage home bakers to invest in a high-quality natural vanilla, such as Nielsen-Massey produces. It is what we use at the shops, and the depth and quality of the flavour is definitely noticeable, especially in recipes like this vanilla macaron.

MACARON SHELLS

Prepare 1 batch (page 152), following the Vanilla variation (page 154)

CLASSIC VANILLA BUTTERCREAM

1 cup (prepare ½ batch, page 222, preferably using Madagascar vanilla)

1. When filling the shells, it is fastest and easiest to lay out all the sandwiches in rows on a clean counter with several inches in between each sandwich. Then remove the top shell and place it directly beside the bottom shell. The bottom shell will have the inside facing up and the top shell will have the top facing up. This will ensure that you fill only the bottom shells and that you pair them with the tops that you selected for them earlier.

2. Fit a piping bag with the same tip you used for piping the macarons, and fill it with the classic vanilla buttercream. Pipe a teaspoon-size dollop of classic vanilla buttercream onto each bottom, leaving a small outer edge unfilled. Once all the bottoms are piped, gently replace the tops to create a sandwich. Lift each sandwich and gently apply pressure from both sides to close the sandwich and spread the filling to the edge. Don't press the top down while the macaron is still on the table or the bottom shell will crack.

3. The finished macarons can be stored in an airtight container in the fridge for up to 3 days.

   Recipe is naturally gluten-free.

DOUBLE CHOCOLATE MACARONS

Double chocolate macarons eat more like a truffle than a cookie. Which is probably because they are filled with a dark chocolate truffle filling. The slight bitterness of the cocoa in the shell balances out the overall sweetness of the macaron. Chocolate is the predominant flavour here, as the almond in the shell is eclipsed by the slight bitterness of the cocoa. What remains is the lovely slightly crisp texture of the macaron as it gives way to the chocolate filling upon first bite.

MACARON SHELLS

Prepare 1 batch (page 152), following the Chocolate variation (page 154)

DARK CHOCOLATE GANACHE

1 cup finely chopped dark chocolate (6 ounces)

¾ cup + 1 tablespoon 35% cream

1. To make the dark chocolate ganache, place the chopped chocolate in a medium heatproof bowl; set aside. In a small saucepan over medium heat, bring the cream just to a simmer, then pour the hot cream over the chocolate. Wait for 1 minute, then whisk until the chocolate is melted and the mixture is smooth. Allow the mixture to cool to room temperature.

2. When filling the shells, it is fastest and easiest to lay out all the sandwiches in rows on a clean counter with several inches in between each sandwich. Then remove the top shell and place it directly beside the bottom shell. The bottom shell will have the inside facing up and the top shell will have the top facing up. This will ensure that you fill only the bottom shells and that you pair them with the tops that you selected for them earlier.

3. Fit a piping bag with the same tip you used for piping the macarons, and fill it with the chocolate ganache. Pipe a teaspoon-size dollop of chocolate ganache onto each bottom, leaving a small outer edge unfilled. Once all the bottoms are piped, gently replace the tops to create a sandwich. Lift each sandwich and gently apply pressure from both sides to close the sandwich and spread the filling to the edge. Don't press the top down while the macaron is still on the table or the bottom shell will crack.

4. The finished macarons can be stored in an airtight container in the fridge for up to 3 days.

Recipe is naturally gluten-free.

CHOCOLATE HAZELNUT MACARONS

You will hear us singing the praises of gianduja a number of times in this book. Chocolate and hazelnut are a match made in heaven, and never was this more true than in the case of chocolate hazelnut macarons. The gianduja ganache is the star of this pairing, but the macaron shell, enhanced with toasted hazelnuts to provide texture an additional flavour, is the perfect vehicle.

MACARON SHELLS

Prepare 1 batch (page 152), following the Hazelnut variation (page 154)

CHOCOLATE HAZELNUT GANACHE

¾ cup finely chopped gianduja (hazelnut chocolate) (4 ounces)

⅓ cup finely chopped dark chocolate (2 ounces)

½ cup 35% cream

1. To make the chocolate hazelnut ganache, place the chopped hazelnut chocolate and dark chocolate in a medium heatproof bowl; set aside. In a small saucepan over medium heat, bring the cream just to a simmer, then pour the hot cream over the chocolate. Wait for 1 minute, then whisk until the chocolate is melted and the mixture is smooth. Allow the mixture to cool to room temperature.

2. When filling the shells, it is fastest and easiest to lay out all the sandwiches in rows on a clean counter with several inches in between each sandwich. Then remove the top shell and place it directly beside the bottom shell. The bottom shell will have the inside facing up and the top shell will have the top facing up. This will ensure that you fill only the bottom shells and that you pair them with the tops that you selected for them earlier.

3. Fit a piping bag with the same tip you used for piping the macarons, and fill it with the chocolate ganache. Pipe a teaspoon-size dollop of chocolate ganache onto each bottom, leaving a small outer edge unfilled. Once all the bottoms are piped, gently replace the tops to create a sandwich. Lift each sandwich and gently apply pressure from both sides to close the sandwich and spread the filling to the edge. Don't press the top down while the macaron is still on the table or the bottom shell will crack.

4. The finished macarons can be stored in an airtight container in the fridge for up to 3 days.

SALTED CARAMEL MACARONS

Many people say salted caramel is their favourite macaron, and for good reason. The balance of salty caramel and the intensely sweet almond shell is intoxicating. When we started making macarons, it took us several months of tweaking to figure out the secrets of the world's foremost salted caramel macaron makers. The key to success is twofold. First, the caramel should be a handmade dry-sugar caramel, which has a more developed flavour than store-bought caramel. Second, adding a touch of coffee extract to the shell subtly enhances that caramel flavour.

MACARON SHELLS

Prepare 1 batch (page 152), following the Salted Caramel variation (page 154)

SALTED CARAMEL FILLING

1 cup salted caramel sauce (page 190)

⅓ cup unsalted butter, room temperature

Tip

There will be some caramel sauce left over after you make the filling. It can be stored for up to 2 weeks. It's great for topping ice cream or mixing into Greek yogurt.

1. In the bowl of a stand mixer fitted with the paddle attachment, beat the caramel sauce and butter on medium speed until light and fluffy like a buttercream.

2. When filling the shells, it is fastest and easiest to lay out all the sandwiches in rows on a clean counter with several inches in between each sandwich. Then remove the top shell and place it directly beside the bottom shell. The bottom shell will have the inside facing up and the top shell will have the top facing up. This will ensure that you fill only the bottom shells and that you pair them with the tops that you selected for them earlier.

3. Fit a piping bag with the same tip you used for piping the macarons, and fill it with the salted caramel filling. Pipe a teaspoon-size dollop of salted caramel filling onto each bottom, leaving a small outer edge unfilled. Once all the bottoms are piped, gently replace the tops to create a sandwich. Lift each sandwich and gently apply pressure from both sides to close the sandwich and spread the filling to the edge. Don't press the top down while the macaron is still on the table or the bottom shell will crack.

4. The finished macarons can be stored in an airtight container in the fridge for up to 3 days.

   Recipe is naturally gluten-free.

EARL GREY
MACARONS

In much of baking, when chocolate is called for we opt for the richness of dark. However, one exception is this tea-infused macaron. Creamy milk chocolate brings out the slightly perfumed notes of Earl Grey. We recommend sourcing a good loose-leaf variety to really enhance the flavour of the chocolate.

MACARON SHELLS

Prepare 1 batch (page 152), following the Earl Grey variation (page 154)

EARL GREY GANACHE

1 cup finely chopped milk chocolate (6 ounces)

½ cup 35% cream

1 teaspoon corn syrup

3 tablespoons loose Earl Grey tea leaves

1½ teaspoon unsalted butter, room temperature

1. To make the Earl Grey ganache, place the chopped chocolate in a medium heatproof bowl; set aside. In a small saucepan over medium heat, bring the cream and corn syrup just to a simmer, stirring occasionally. Remove from the heat and add the tea leaves. Cover the pot with plastic wrap and set aside to steep and cool to room temperature.

2. Strain the steeped cream through a fine-mesh sieve into a small bowl, discarding the tea leaves. In the same pot, bring the cream just to a simmer, then pour the hot cream over the chocolate. Wait for 1 minute, then whisk until the chocolate is melted and the mixture is smooth. Whisk in the butter until incorporated. Allow the ganache to cool to room temperature.

3. When filling the shells, it is fastest and easiest to lay out all the sandwiches in rows on a clean counter with several inches in between each sandwich. Then remove the top shell and place it directly beside the bottom shell. The bottom shell will have the inside facing up and the top shell will have the top facing up. This will ensure that you fill only the bottom shells and that you pair them with the tops that you selected for them earlier.

4. Fit a piping bag with the same tip you used for piping the macarons, and fill it with the Earl Grey ganache. Pipe a teaspoon-size dollop of Earl Grey ganache onto each bottom, leaving a small outer edge unfilled. Once all the bottoms are piped, gently replace the tops to create a sandwich. Lift each sandwich and gently apply pressure from both sides to close the sandwich and spread the filling to the edge. Don't press the top down while the macaron is still on the table or the bottom shell will crack.

5. The finished macarons can be stored in an airtight container in the fridge for up to 3 days.

PISTACHIO CREAM MACARONS

We feel very passionate about our pistachio macarons. Pistachio is a particularly popular flavouring for many sweets, including gelato and truffles, but often these items are flavoured in part with almond. Pure pistachio paste is extremely expensive, so sweet purveyors will often use a mix of pistachios and almonds to reduce costs. We use only 100 percent pure pistachio paste in the filling for our pistachio macarons, and we highly recommend you do the same at home. The difference in taste is profound—and highly addictive.

MACARON SHELLS

Prepare 1 batch (page 152), following the Pistachio variation (page 154)

PISTACHIO FILLING

1 cup Classic Vanilla Buttercream (prepare ½ batch, page 222); use at room temperature

1 tablespoon pure pistachio paste

1. To make the pistachio filling, in a medium bowl, whisk together the buttercream and pistachio paste until thoroughly combined.

2. When filling the shells, it is fastest and easiest to lay out all the sandwiches in rows on a clean counter with several inches in between each sandwich. Then remove the top shell and place it directly beside the bottom shell. The bottom shell will have the inside facing up and the top shell will have the top facing up. This will ensure that you fill only the bottom shells and that you pair them with the tops that you selected for them earlier.

3. Fit a piping bag with the same tip you used for piping the macarons, and fill it with the pistachio filling. Pipe a teaspoon-size dollop of pistachio filling onto each bottom, leaving a small outer edge unfilled. Once all the bottoms are piped, gently replace the tops to create a sandwich. Lift each sandwich and gently apply pressure from both sides to close the sandwich and spread the filling to the edge. Don't press the top down while the macaron is still on the table or the bottom shell will crack.

4. The finished macarons can be stored in an airtight container in the fridge for up to 3 days.

Recipe is naturally gluten-free.

RASPBERRY MACARONS

We have noticed a couple of things at the shop over the years. First, children today have a more advanced palate than we did growing up. It is so sweet to watch them come into the shops and make a beeline for the French macaron display. It reminds us of staring longingly through the glass display at the local Baskin-Robbins when we were kids. It's also fun to see that, with few exceptions, most children under the age of five want "the pink one," which is our raspberry macaron. There is something so appealing about the soft pink colour and the slightly tart berry taste that children love. And we have to confess, now that we've graduated from the 31 flavours, we like them a fair bit ourselves.

MACARON SHELLS

Prepare 1 batch (page 152), following the Raspberry variation (page 154)

RASPBERRY FILLING

1 cup Classic Vanilla Buttercream (prepare ½ batch, page 222); use at room temperature

¼ cup Raspberry Purée (prepare ½ batch, page 245, or see source guide, page 248)

1. To make the raspberry filling, in a medium bowl, whisk together the buttercream and raspberry purée until thoroughly combined.

2. When filling the shells, it is fastest and easiest to lay out all the sandwiches in rows on a clean counter with several inches in between each sandwich. Then remove the top shell and place it directly beside the bottom shell. The bottom shell will have the inside facing up and the top shell will have the top facing up. This will ensure that you fill only the bottom shells and that you pair them with the tops that you selected for them earlier.

3. Fit a piping bag with the same tip you used for piping the macarons, and fill it with the raspberry filling. Pipe a teaspoon-size dollop of raspberry filling onto each bottom, leaving a small outer edge unfilled. Once all the bottoms are piped, gently replace the tops to create a sandwich. Lift each sandwich and gently apply pressure from both sides to close the sandwich and spread the filling to the edge. Don't press the top down while the macaron is still on the table or the bottom shell will crack.

4. The finished macarons can be stored in an airtight container in the fridge for up to 3 days.

Recipe is naturally gluten-free.

DESSERT-SIZED
TIRAMISÙ MACARONS

In France, the famous pastry chef Pierre Hermé makes several dessert-sized macarons that feature a large version of the traditional shell paired with several complementary fillings. We loved this idea of promoting the macaron to a full-size plated dessert and were excited to play around with traditional desserts like tiramisù. In our version, two large salted caramel macaron shells sandwich a filling of dark chocolate ganache and light espresso pastry cream.

MACARON SHELLS

Prepare 1 batch (page 152), following the Salted Caramel variation (page 154) and piping 3-inch rounds

DARK CHOCOLATE GANACHE

Prepare 1 batch (page 156)

COFFEE PASTRY CREAM

½ cup + 2 tablespoons whole milk

1 tablespoon finely ground espresso beans (not instant)

2 large egg yolks

¼ cup granulated sugar

2 tablespoons cornstarch

1½ teaspoons pure vanilla extract

1 teaspoon unsalted butter, room temperature

¼ cup 35% cream

¼ cup mascarpone cheese

1. To make the coffee pastry cream, combine the milk and ground espresso beans in a small saucepan over medium heat and bring just to a simmer. Remove from the heat, cover the pot with plastic wrap and set aside to steep and cool to room temperature.

2. Strain the infused milk a fine-mesh sieve into a small bowl, discarding the coffee grounds. Return the milk to the pot and again bring it just to a simmer.

3. In a medium bowl, whisk together the egg yolks, sugar, cornstarch and vanilla until smooth. Slowly pour a thin, steady stream of hot milk into the egg yolk mixture, whisking all the while. Do not pour the hot milk in all at once or the eggs will scramble.

4. Pour the tempered mixture back into the pot and bring it to a boil over medium heat, whisking constantly. Cook, whisking constantly, until the pastry cream thickens, about 1 to 2 minutes.

5. Strain the pastry cream through a fine-mesh sieve into a bowl. (This will remove any egg bits that accidentally cooked too quickly.) Stir in the butter until fully incorporated. Place plastic wrap directly on the surface of the pastry cream to prevent a skin from forming and chill completely in the fridge, 2 to 3 hours.

6. In a small bowl, whisk together the 35% cream and mascarpone cheese until the mixture thickens and holds soft peaks. Do not overmix or the cream will take on a curdled look. Stir the pastry cream to loosen it, then fold in the mascarpone cream in two stages. (This lightens the pastry cream.)

7. When filling the shells, it is fastest and easiest to lay out all the sandwiches in rows on a clean counter with several inches in between each sandwich. Then remove the top shell and place it directly beside the bottom shell. The bottom shell will have the inside facing up and the top shell will have the top facing up. This will ensure that you fill only the bottom shells and that you pair them with the tops that you selected for them earlier.

8. Fit a piping bag with the same tip you used for piping the macarons, and fill it with the chocolate ganache. Pipe a ring of ganache $^1/_2$-inch tall around the outer edge

of each bottom shell. Spoon the pastry cream inside the ring of ganache. It should rise above the ganache approximately $1/2$-inch.

9. Once all the bottoms are filled, gently replace the tops to create sandwiches. Lift each sandwich and gently apply pressure from both sides to close the sandwich. Don't press the top down while the macaron is still on the table or the bottom shell will crack.

10. The finished macarons can be stored in an airtight container in the fridge for up to 3 days.

Recipe is naturally gluten-free.

MINT CHOCOLATE MACARONS

When we introduced this macaron at the shop for the holiday season one year, it was such a hit that it became one of our regular year-round offerings. The mint is refreshing, while the dark chocolate ganache balances out the sweetness of the macaron.

MACARON SHELLS

Prepare 1 batch (page 152), following the Mint Chocolate variation (page 154)

MINT CHOCOLATE GANACHE

1 cup finely chopped dark chocolate (6 ounces)

¾ cup + 1 tablespoon 35% cream

1 teaspoon peppermint extract

1. To make the mint chocolate ganache, place the chopped chocolate in a medium heatproof bowl; set aside. In a small saucepan over medium heat, bring the cream just to a simmer, then pour the hot cream over the chocolate. Wait for 1 minute, then add the peppermint extract and whisk until the chocolate is melted and the mixture is smooth. Allow the mixture to cool to room temperature.

2. When filling the shells, it is fastest and easiest to lay out all the sandwiches in rows on a clean counter with several inches in between each sandwich. Then remove the top shell and place it directly beside the bottom shell. The bottom shell will have the inside facing up and the top shell will have the top facing up. This will ensure that you fill only the bottom shells and that you pair them with the tops that you selected for them earlier.

3. Fit a piping bag with the same tip you used for piping the macarons, and fill it with the mint chocolate ganache. Pipe a teaspoon-size dollop of mint chocolate ganache onto each bottom, leaving a small outer edge unfilled. Once all the bottoms are piped, gently replace the tops to create a sandwich. Lift each sandwich and gently apply pressure from both sides to close the sandwich and spread the filling to the edge. Don't press the top down while the macaron is still on the table or the bottom shell will crack.

4. The finished macarons can be stored in an airtight container in the fridge for up to 3 days.

   Recipe is naturally gluten-free.

7

CHILLED
CRÈME DESSERTS

DRUNKEN MIXED BERRY PAVLOVAS

Pavlova was created in the 1920s as a special dessert for the famous ballerina Anna Pavlova. We are not sure whether it was intentional, but it is entirely fitting that the dessert, which consists of cooked meringue, soft, fluffy whipped cream and macerated berries, is as light as air, much like the dancer herself. Cornstarch and vinegar give the meringue its crisp outer crust and softer chewy centre. The rich whipped cream and the berries infused with Grand Marnier balance out the intense sweetness of the meringue and provide the overall sense of decadence.

4 large egg whites, room temperature

¼ teaspoon salt

1¼ cups granulated sugar

2 teaspoons cornstarch

2 teaspoons white vinegar

2 teaspoons pure vanilla extract

½ pint strawberries, hulled, halved or quartered if large

½ pint blueberries

½ pint raspberries

½ pint blackberries

3 tablespoons Grand Marnier

1¼ cups 35% cream

½ lemon, for garnish

Fresh mint leaves, for garnish

Recipe is naturally gluten-free.

Recipe is naturally dairy-free if served without the cream.

Tip

When whipping any meringue, remember to start with a spotlessly clean, dry bowl. Any fat residue will prevent the meringue from whipping.

1. Preheat the oven to 300°F. Line a baking sheet with parchment paper. Using a 5-inch round cookie cutter as a guide, trace 6 circles, about 2 inches apart, onto the paper with a pencil. Turn the paper pencil side down.

2. In the bowl of a stand mixer fitted with the whisk attachment, beat the egg whites and salt on medium speed until soft peaks form. Increase the speed to medium-high and add 1 cup of the sugar, ⅓ cup at a time, beating until the meringue is glossy and holds stiff peaks.

3. Remove the bowl from the mixer. Sprinkle in the cornstarch, vinegar and vanilla and gently fold to combine.

4. Dip a large spoon into a glass of hot water, scoop up a heaping spoonful of meringue and drop it in the centre of one of the pencilled circles. Continue dipping and scooping until you have six equal mounds of meringue. Dip the spoon in the hot water again and use the back of the spoon to evenly spread one meringue out toward the edges of the circle; repeat with the remaining meringues. Dip the spoon again, and use the back of the spoon to gently create a shallow crater in the centre of each meringue, as if you were forming a nest.

5. Place the meringues in the oven and immediately reduce the temperature to 250°F. Bake for 1 hour and 15 minutes or until the meringues are hard and dry on the outside but have a slightly soft centre. They should remain white. The meringues may need to be baked longer if the weather is more humid. Turn off the oven and let the meringues cool completely in the oven. The unfilled meringue nests can be stored in an airtight container at room temperature for up to 1 week.

6. Half an hour before serving, in a large bowl, lightly toss together the berries, the remaining ¼ cup sugar and the Grand Marnier. Let the berries macerate for 30 minutes, until the sugar dissolves and the berry juices begin to run.

7. Just before serving, whip the cream to soft peaks. Place each of the meringues on a dessert plate and top with whipped cream, then top with macerated berries. Garnish with a mint leaf and a gentle squeeze of lemon.

RASPBERRY AND VANILLA LAYERED PANNA COTTA

Berries and cream are a classic pairing in many desserts. Berries with ice cream, layered with cream in a pavlova or combined with custard on a fruit tart—all play on the pleasing contrast of the rich cream and the tartness of fresh berries. But no dessert captures this essence more purely and directly than a layered panna cotta. The simplicity of this classic Italian dessert allows the ingredients to shine, and this is only reinforced by the beauty of the coloured layers. As we were test baking for this book, we would often drop off leftovers to friends and family at the end of the day, and this panna cotta received rave reviews across the board. In chatting with these friends, we discovered that many people hadn't tried panna cotta, and they were so pleasantly surprised by the simple dessert that several of them asked for the recipe before the book came out.

VANILLA PANNA COTTA

1 tablespoon unflavoured gelatin (1 envelope)

1½ cups 35% cream

½ cup whole milk

¼ cup granulated sugar

1 teaspoon pure vanilla extract

RASPBERRY PANNA COTTA

1½ teaspoons unflavoured gelatin (½ envelope)

½ cup 35% cream

¼ cup whole milk

½ cup Raspberry Purée (prepare 1 batch, page 245)

2 tablespoons granulated sugar

½ teaspoon pure vanilla extract

RASPBERRY GELÉE

1½ teaspoons unflavoured gelatin (½ envelope)

1 cup Raspberry Purée (prepare a double batch, page 245)

2 teaspoons granulated sugar

1. To make the vanilla panna cotta, soften the gelatin according to the instructions on the envelope. In a small saucepan, whisk together the cream, milk, sugar and vanilla. Gently heat the mixture over medium heat, stirring, until hot to the touch and the sugar has dissolved. Do not let boil. Remove from the heat and whisk in the softened gelatin until it has fully dissolved.

2. Half fill a large bowl with ice and add a little water. Place the saucepan in the bowl so that it rests on top of the ice. Allow the panna cotta to cool, whisking gently (so you don't introduce air bubbles) now and again, until thickened slightly, about 15 minutes. Divide the panna cotta evenly between 6 to 8 dessert glasses. Refrigerate until fully set, 1 to 2 hours.

3. When the vanilla panna cotta is set, prepare the raspberry panna cotta, repeating steps 1 and 2, and including the raspberry purée in the cream mixture. Divide the raspberry panna cotta evenly on top of the vanilla panna cotta and return to the fridge to set for 1 to 2 hours.

4. Once the panna cottas have set, prepare the raspberry gelée. Soften the gelatin according to the instructions on the envelope. In a small saucepan over medium heat, gently heat the raspberry purée with the sugar, stirring occasionally, until hot to the touch. Remove from the heat, add the prepared gelatin and whisk until fully dissolved. Cool the gelée over the ice bath, whisking occasionally, until cooled, 10 to 15 minutes.

5. Divide the gelée evenly on top of the panna cottas. Return to the fridge to set once more, for 1 to 2 hours. Serve chilled. The panna cottas can be stored, covered, in the fridge for up to 3 days.

Recipe is naturally gluten-free.

CLASSIC VANILLA CRÈME BRÛLÉE

Crème brûlée is the ultimate in decadent desserts. The sheer joy of sitting down to consume what is essentially a sugar-encrusted cup of baked sweetened cream is a rare pleasure in adulthood. One might think, given its simplicity, that crème brûlée could be whipped up without too much attention, but it is often the simplest desserts that require the most skill and care. The sugar should be fully dissolved, the egg custard cooked but not grainy, and the caramelized sugar golden but not burnt. When attention is given to each of these elements, the result is a smooth and silky custard that makes it obvious why this has been a favourite dessert since the seventeenth century.

2 cups 35% cream

5 large egg yolks

¼ cup + 5 tablespoons granulated sugar

2 teaspoons pure vanilla extract

Tip

To prevent your cream from burning when you heat it, rinse your saucepan with water, then drain the water out but do not dry the pan. The "lick" of water in the bottom will create a barrier between the pot and the cream to prevent burning.

1. Preheat the oven to 325°F. Place the ramekins in a deep baking pan.

2. In a medium saucepan over medium-high heat, bring the cream just to a simmer. Meanwhile, in a medium bowl, whisk together the egg yolks, ¼ cup of the granulated sugar and the vanilla until well blended. Add the hot cream in a thin, steady stream, while whisking constantly. Do not add the hot cream too quickly or the eggs will scramble. Strain the custard through a fine-mesh sieve into a bowl. Using a spoon, skim off any bubbles from the surface of the custard.

3. Divide the custard evenly between the ramekins. Cover the baking pan with tin foil to create a seal and poke 4 or 5 holes in the top with a toothpick. Gently place the baking pan in the oven. Peel back a corner of the foil and add enough boiling water to the pan to come halfway up the sides of the ramekins. Reseal the foil and bake for 30 to 40 minutes or until the custards are just set around the edge but the centres jiggle slightly when you gently nudge the pan. Check the custards in the last 5 to 10 minutes of baking to ensure that they are not overbaking. If they look soupy, bake a few minutes longer.

4. Carefully remove the baking pan from the oven, uncover the custards and allow them to cool to room temperature in the water, then remove them from the baking pan and place them in the fridge to set for at least 2 to 3 hours. The custards can be stored in the fridge, covered, for up to 3 days.

5. When ready to serve, evenly sprinkle 1 tablespoon of the granulated sugar on the top of each custard. Using a kitchen blowtorch, pass the flame over the sugar in quick swirling motions until the sugar is caramelized. Alternatively, you can place the ramekins on a baking sheet and broil them until caramelized, 30 seconds to 1 minute, watching carefully so the sugar does not burn. Allow the puddings to stand for a few minutes until the caramel is hardened before serving.

Recipe is naturally gluten-free.

CHOCOLATE PEANUT
BUTTER PARFAITS

We couldn't write a cookbook and not include a parfait, that chilled dessert that allows us to layer our favourite mousses and fillings and intersperse them with a variety of toppings for texture. Here we've opted for the much-loved combination of chocolate and peanut butter, but we add bits of toffee for crunch and some candied hazelnuts that we hope you will have fun making at home. This is an excellent dessert to make with the kids. Set it up like a sundae bar so they can layer their own parfaits. All sorts of toppings work well with these mousses, so feel free to get creative with toppings and garnishes.

MILK CHOCOLATE MOUSSE

⅔ cup whole milk

3 large egg yolks

1 teaspoon pure vanilla extract

⅛ teaspoon salt

12 ounces milk chocolate, chopped
(or 2 cups milk chocolate chips)

1 cup 35% cream

PEANUT BUTTER MOUSSE

½ cup plain cream cheese, room
temperature

½ cup smooth peanut butter

⅓ cup icing sugar, sifted

2 teaspoons pure vanilla extract

¾ cup 35% cream

GARNISHES

½ cup chocolate sauce (Chocolate Glaze,
page 239, or store-bought)

Caramelized Hazelnuts (prepare 1 batch,
page 247)

1 cup toffee bits

½ cup salted roasted peanuts, coarsely
chopped

1 cup semisweet chocolate chips or shavings

1. To make the milk chocolate mousse, in a medium saucepan over medium heat, bring the milk just to a simmer. Meanwhile, in a medium bowl, whisk together the egg yolks, vanilla and salt. Add the hot milk in a thin, steady stream, whisking constantly to prevent cooking the eggs.

2. Pour the mixture back into the pot and cook over low heat, stirring constantly, until the custard thickens slightly, about 3 minutes. Remove from the heat, add the chopped chocolate and stir until melted and smooth. Set aside to cool to room temperature.

3. Whip the cream until soft peaks form. Gently fold half of the cream into the chocolate custard just until combined, then fold in the other half, taking care not to overmix the mousse.

4. Fit a piping bag with a large round tip, then fill with the chocolate mousse. Pipe the mousse evenly into the dessert cups, filling them about one-third full. Top with some of the toffee bits and chopped peanuts. Put the dessert cups in the fridge to chill while you make the peanut butter mousse.

5. To make the peanut butter mousse, in the bowl of a stand mixer fitted with the paddle attachment, beat the cream cheese and peanut butter on medium speed until well blended and smooth, about 3 minutes. Add the icing sugar and beat on medium-low until incorporated. Stop the mixer to scrape down the sides of the bowl. Add the vanilla and beat to combine.

6. Whip the cream until soft peaks form. Gently fold half of the whipped cream into the peanut butter mixture just until combined, then fold in the other half, taking care not to overmix the mousse. Gentle folding is the key.

7. Fit a piping bag with a large round tip, then fill with the peanut butter mousse. Pipe half the mousse evenly between the dessert cups. Top with the chocolate chips or shavings, then pipe the remaining mousse on top. Serve immediately, garnished with chocolate sauce, caramelized hazelnuts and additional toppings of your choice.

Recipe is naturally gluten-free.

GREEK YOGURT, HONEY & FRUIT POPS

Anybody who knows us also knows that we subscribe to the French tradition of pastry—that is, you can never use too much butter. However, they also know that we temper all our rich treats with balanced meals and healthy snacks. As much as we love our crème brûlée and buttercreams, we also love yogurt and berries. These pops are super easy to make and a treat you can enjoy often. We're partial to frozen mixed berries, but you can use any fruit combination you like (we think banana-strawberry is particularly good). You will need 12 popsicle moulds for this recipe.

1½ cups frozen fruit

3 cups plain full-fat Greek yogurt

¾ cup honey

1 teaspoon pure vanilla extract

Tip

We've used honey as a sweetener, but you can also use an equal amount of agave syrup or a touch of maple syrup.

1. Place the frozen fruit in a bowl and allow it to thaw for 20 minutes.

2. Place the softened fruit and its juices in a blender and add the Greek yogurt, honey and vanilla. Blitz on high speed until the mixture is smooth and all the fruit is thoroughly blended. Pour the mixture into popsicle moulds, insert wooden popsicle sticks and freeze until firm, 4 to 6 hours.

3. To remove the popsicles from their moulds, dip the mould into a bowl of hot water for a few seconds at a time until the popsicles loosen enough to pull them out. Take care not to melt the popsicles while doing so! The popsicles can be frozen for up to 1 week.

Recipe is naturally gluten-free.

FRENCH CREAM PUFFS
with Craquelin Tops

We have been making cream puffs for years but are fairly new to making this variety. We were pleasantly surprised to find that the craquelin top makes for a more stable and uniform cream puff. The key to a successful pâte à choux is the air pocket that forms during baking, which allows the cream puffs to be filled with a variety of delicious fillings. The craquelin top helps with creating this pocket and is worth the extra step. It also looks beautiful!

CRAQUELIN TOPS

6½ tablespoons unsalted butter, room temperature

¼ cup packed brown sugar

¼ cup + 2 tablespoons all-purpose flour

PÂTE À CHOUX (CREAM PUFF PASTRY)

½ cup water

½ cup whole milk

½ cup unsalted butter

1 tablespoon granulated sugar

1 teaspoon salt

1 cup bread flour

4 large eggs

VANILLA PASTRY CREAM

Prepare 1 batch (page 243)

CHOCOLATE GLAZE

Prepare 1 batch (page 239)

Tip

Try different fillings, like lemon curd, chocolate mousse or toffee pastry cream. If you are pressed for time, leave off the craquelin top and dip the tops of the baked puffs in melted chocolate.

1. Put oven racks in the upper and lower thirds of the oven and preheat the oven to 350°F.

2. To make the craquelin tops, in a medium bowl and using a rubber spatula, cream the butter and brown sugar until well combined. Add the flour and blend until well combined and the dough is smooth. Roll the dough out between 2 sheets of parchment paper until it is ⅛-inch thick. Slide the dough onto a baking sheet and chill in the freezer while you prepare the cream puffs.

3. To make the pâte à choux, line 2 baking sheets with parchment paper. In a medium saucepan over medium heat, bring the water, milk, butter, sugar and salt to a boil. Remove from the heat, add the flour all at once and stir vigorously with a wooden spoon until a dough forms. Return to the heat and cook, stirring constantly, until the dough pulls away from the sides and bottom of the saucepan.

4. Transfer the dough to the bowl of a stand mixer fitted with the paddle attachment and beat on medium speed for 1 to 2 minutes to release some of the heat. (This will ensure that the eggs will not scramble when they're added to the dough.) Add the eggs one at a time, beating well after each addition and stopping the mixer after each addition to scrape down the sides of the bowl. The finished dough should have a smooth texture and light sheen and be firm enough to hold its shape when piped.

5. Transfer the batter to a piping bag fitted with a ½-inch round tip. Pipe 12 rounds onto each baking sheet, leaving lots of space around them.

6. Using a round cookie cutter slightly smaller than the piped puffs, cut out rounds from the craquelin. Place a round on top of each piped puff.

7. Bake for 25 minutes or until the tops are golden and the sides are crisp when pressed. For even baking, rotate the pans front to back and top to bottom halfway through. Allow the cream puffs to cool completely on the baking sheets.

8. Fit a piping bag with a ½-inch round tip and fill with the pastry cream. Insert the tip into the bottom of each cream puff and gently squeeze to fill the air pocket with cream. Spoon a dollop of chocolate glaze onto the top of each cream puff and place in the fridge to set for 10 minutes. The filled cream puffs should be eaten the same day, but unfilled cream puffs can be frozen in an airtight container for up to 2 weeks.

MACARON ICE-CREAM SUNDAE SANDWICHES

We can't take credit for the ingenious idea of turning a French macaron into an ice-cream sandwich. That pastry honour, as usual, goes to France. We can, however, put our over-the-top North American twist on it. After all, if there's one thing we know on this side of the pond, it's ice cream.

FRENCH MACARON SHELLS

Prepare 1 batch (page 152), piping twenty 3-inch rounds

FILLINGS

Ice cream (½ cup of a chosen flavour for each sandwich)

1 cup each of a variety of candies, nuts and chocolate chips (if desired)

Tip

If you are not serving immediately, wrap the finished ice-cream sandwiches in individual parchment wrappers and freeze so you can grab them as desired.

1. Lay out all the sandwiches in rows on a clean counter with several inches in between each sandwich. Then remove the top shell and place it directly beside the bottom shell. The bottom shell will have the inside facing up and the top shell will have the top facing up.

2. Scoop ½ cup of ice cream onto each bottom shell. Using the back of a spoon, gently press the ice cream out to the edges. Replace the tops to create a sandwich.

3. If desired, spread your chosen candies, nuts or chocolate chips evenly in a shallow dish, then roll the ice cream edge of each sandwich through the toppings to add flavour and texture.

MANGO CHEESECAKE

Bursting with flavour, this mango cheesecake is a decisive salute to the tropical mango. The rich cream cheese is the perfect vehicle for the sweetness of the fruit. Our friend Liz, who is from the Caribbean, often makes this for special events and parties, and we fell in love with it. It is a family recipe of hers and we are grateful that she has allowed us to include it in this book. Many of our recipes come from our families and our childhoods, so we're always excited to include someone else's cherished recipes. You will need to bake the cheesecake the day before serving.

CRUST

1½ cups graham cracker crumbs

2 tablespoons granulated sugar

¼ cup unsalted butter, melted

FILLING

3 packages (250 g each) cream cheese, room temperature

¼ cup all-purpose flour

Zest of 1 lemon

1 teaspoon pure vanilla extract

3 large eggs

⅔ cup mango purée

¾ cup granulated sugar

½ cup mango purée, for garnish (optional)

Tip

To make the fancy garnish in the photo, just before serving, peel and very thinly slice 6 large mangoes (for the large cheesecake) or 8 large mangoes (2 for each 4-inch cheesecake). Roll up one slice in a spiral and stand it up in the centre of the cheesecake. Arrange the remaining slices, slightly overlapping them in a circular pattern, all the way to the edges of the cheesecake.

1. Preheat the oven to 325°F. To make the springform pan watertight, wrap the outside with tin foil.

2. To make the crust, in a bowl, stir together the graham cracker crumbs and sugar. Add the melted butter and stir until well combined. Pack the mixture firmly and evenly into bottom of the springform pan. Chill in the freezer while you make the filling.

3. To make the filling, in the bowl of a stand mixer fitted with the paddle attachment, beat the cream cheese on medium-high speed for 3 minutes, until smooth. Turn the mixer to low speed and add the flour and lemon zest, stopping to scrape down the sides of the bowl at least once.

4. Increase the speed to medium and beat in the vanilla, then add the eggs one at a time, beating well after each addition. Scrape down the sides of the bowl, then add the ⅔ cup mango purée and beat until combined. Add the sugar and beat on medium-high speed for 30 seconds.

5. Pour the batter over the crust. Set the springform pan in a deep baking pan and place in the oven. Add hot water to come halfway up the side of the springform pan to create a water bath.

6. Bake for 50 to 60 minutes or until the top is firm to the touch but the centre has a slight jiggle. Turn off the oven and leave the cheesecake in for 1 hour, with the oven door slightly ajar.

7. Remove the cheesecake from the water bath and allow it to cool completely on a wire rack. Cover with plastic wrap and place in the fridge to set overnight before removing the sides of the pan.

8. Before serving, top the cheesecake with ½ cup mango purée, spreading it evenly with a small offset spatula. Or try your hand at the mango flower garnish in the tip. Serve chilled. The cheesecake can be stored in the fridge, covered, for up to 5 days.

CLASSIC VANILLA CHEESECAKE

In many ways, plain vanilla cheesecake acts as a blank canvas, and for this reason, the quality of ingredients and the correct method are key to achieving a slightly dense yet silky smooth texture. For this recipe we recommend using Philadelphia-brand cream cheese, as it has always provided the best result for us. The sour cream in the filling makes this more of a New York–style cheesecake. We haven't dictated a topping for this cake because it pairs so well with so many garnishes, including fruit coulis, chocolate glaze and dulce de leche. You will need to bake the cheesecake the day before serving.

CRUST

1½ cups graham cracker crumbs

2 tablespoons granulated sugar

¼ cup unsalted butter, melted

FILLING

3 packages (250 g each) cream cheese, room temperature

¼ cup all-purpose flour

Zest of 1 lemon

1 teaspoon pure vanilla extract

3 large eggs

½ cup sour cream

¾ cup granulated sugar

Tip

Three keys to preventing your cheesecake from cracking are: not overbaking, allowing it to cool partially in the oven, and making sure it is fully cooled before chilling in the fridge.

1. Preheat the oven to 325°F. To make the springform pan watertight, wrap the outside with tin foil.

2. To make the crust, in a bowl, stir together the graham cracker crumbs and sugar. Add the melted butter and stir until well combined. Pack the mixture firmly and evenly into the bottom of the springform pan. Chill in the freezer while you make the filling.

3. To make the filling, in the bowl of a stand mixer fitted with the paddle attachment, beat the cream cheese on medium-high speed for 3 minutes, until smooth. Turn the mixer to low speed and add the flour and lemon zest, stopping to scrape down the sides of the bowl at least once.

4. Increase the speed to medium and beat in the vanilla, then add the eggs one at a time, beating well after each addition. Scrape down the sides of the bowl, then add the sour cream and beat until combined. Add the sugar and beat on medium-high speed for 30 seconds.

5. Pour the filling onto the crust. Set the springform pan in a deep baking pan and place in the oven. Add hot water to come halfway up the side of the springform pan to create a water bath.

6. Bake for 50 to 60 minutes or until the top is firm to the touch but the centre has a slight jiggle. Turn off the oven and leave the cheesecake in for 1 hour, with the oven door slightly ajar.

7. Remove the cheesecake from the water bath and allow it to cool completely on a wire rack. Cover with plastic wrap and place in the fridge to set overnight before removing the sides of the pan. Serve chilled. The cheesecake can be stored in the fridge, covered, for up to 5 days.

8

CONFECTIONS AND
SWEETS

SALTED CARAMEL SAUCE

You may have noticed that quite a few recipes in this book make use of this salted caramel sauce. While it is true that there are many store-bought varieties that would suffice, the difference in the flavour and quality of this version is epic. It is a "dry" caramel, in that it begins by slowly caramelizing granulated sugar in a saucepan. This allows the sugar to darken slightly beyond what would be typical, lending a richer, slightly bitter caramel taste. The cream enriches the sauce, and the fleur de sel plays up the salty-sweet tones to add balance. It is equally successful used as both a garnish and a flavouring component, but as the picture illustrates, we think it makes a pretty special gift as well.

2 cups granulated sugar

1 cup 35% cream

½ teaspoon fleur de sel

Tip

Once you have tried the beauty of the original, feel free to experiment by adding flavour extracts such as vanilla, mint or coffee, or even liqueurs.

1. In a medium saucepan, heat ½ cup of the sugar over medium-high heat, stirring constantly so the sugar does not burn. Once the sugar has melted and is a light golden colour, add another ½ cup sugar. Continue to caramelize the sugar, ½ cup at a time, until all the sugar has all been added and the caramel is a deep golden colour.

2. Reduce the heat to medium-low and slowly add the cream, stirring constantly. Be careful, as the steam from the bubbling cream is very hot. Add the salt and continue to cook, stirring occasionally, until all the hard sugar bits have dissolved and the caramel sauce has come to a boil. Remove from the heat and cool before serving. The sauce can be stored in an airtight container in the fridge for up to 2 weeks.

Recipe is naturally gluten-free.

Fleur de Sel
CARAMELS

There is nothing quite like fleur de sel caramels. The rich, buttery caramel base, crunchy little pieces of sea salt and super-chewy texture all combine to form a one-bite revelry in the mouth. Really the only problem is the inability to eat just one, which—trust us—is impossible. We're convinced the small individually wrapped pieces were designed that way less for packaging purposes and more for slowing down speedy little hands. There is always something to be said for classics, and the traditional fleur de sel garnish is pretty much perfection, but we also love the idea of changing up the flavour with a variety of specialty salts, like pink Himalayan or smoked black salt.

4 cups granulated sugar

4 cups 35% cream

2 cups corn syrup

⅔ cup unsalted butter

1 teaspoon salt

2 teaspoons pure vanilla extract

1½ teaspoons fleur de sel

Tip

The key to success when making salted caramels is having an accurate candy thermometer. If the caramel is off by just one or two degrees either way, you will end up with a caramel that is either too soft or too hard to eat.

1. Lightly spray the bottom and sides a 10-inch square baking pan with non-stick cooking spray. Line the sides and bottom with parchment paper, leaving a 1-inch overhang of parchment on the sides.

2. In a medium saucepan, heat the sugar, cream, corn syrup and butter over medium-high heat until the butter is melted, stirring occasionally. Continue cooking the mixture, stirring constantly, until a candy thermometer reads 248°F, about 15 minutes.

3. Remove from the heat and stir in the 1 teaspoon salt and the vanilla. Pour the caramel into the prepared pan. Immediately sprinkle the fleur de sel evenly all over the top. Allow the caramel to cool completely, 2 to 3 hours.

4. Lightly spray a cutting board with non-stick cooking spray. Lift the slab of caramel from the pan and place it on the cutting board. Spray a chef's knife with cooking spray and cut the caramels into 1-inch cubes. Wrap each caramel in parchment paper or waxed paper. The caramels can be stored in an airtight container at room temperature for up to 3 weeks.

Recipe is naturally gluten-free.

ENGLISH TOFFEE
with Toasted Almonds

English toffee is one of several confections we make Bobbette & Belle that was introduced as a seasonal holiday item but was so popular that we continued to make it year round. The crunchy, buttery toffee surrounded by dark chocolate and toasted almonds is pretty much addictive. This is probably one of the reasons it is so often made as a gift item at the holidays. A little goes a long way, and it is the perfect snack for guests to nibble on at seasonal cocktail parties. It stores extremely well and can be made ahead, which makes gift giving a breeze. Keep in mind that it is sensitive to humidity, so store it at room temperature in an airtight container.

1⅔ cups granulated sugar

1½ cups unsalted butter

¼ cup water

2 tablespoons corn syrup

1 tablespoon pure vanilla extract

1½ teaspoons salt

¼ teaspoon baking soda

1½ pound semisweet chocolate, finely chopped (4 cups)

5 cups skin-on almonds, coarsely chopped and toasted (page 12)

Tip

Chocolate has a very low melting point. When melting chocolate, do not let the bowl touch the water or get too hot in the microwave, otherwise the chocolate will burn.

Always store your toffee in an airtight container, as sugar absorbs moisture in the air, turning your toffee soft and chewy.

1. Line 2 baking sheets with parchment paper.

2. In a medium saucepan, combine the sugar, butter, water, corn syrup, vanilla and salt. Bring to a boil over medium-high heat and cook, stirring occasionally, until a candy thermometer reads 300°F, about 15 minutes. Remove from the heat and stir in the baking soda. Immediately pour the toffee onto the lined baking sheets and using a rubber spatula, spread it out until it almost reaches the edges. Allow the toffee to cool completely.

3. Place half the chopped chocolate in a medium bowl and melt over a double boiler or in the microwave. Pour half the melted chocolate over the first sheet of cooled toffee and using a rubber spatula, immediately spread it evenly over the whole surface. Working quickly before the chocolate sets, sprinkle a quarter of the chopped almonds over the chocolate. Repeat with the second sheet of toffee. Let the chocolate and nuts fully set on both sheets, about 8 minutes. Flip both toffee sheets over onto the counter or other baking sheets and lift off the parchment.

4. Melt the other half of the chocolate in the same bowl over a double boiler or in the microwave, and repeat the coating procedure for both toffee sheets, sprinkling with the remaining almonds. Allow the coated toffee to fully set before breaking into pieces and packaging or eating. The finished toffee can be stored in an airtight container at room temperature for up to 2 months.

Recipe is naturally gluten-free.

PEANUT BRITTLE

We had never really thought about making peanut brittle until Roots Canada approached us to make some items for their Canada-wide holiday general stores. One of the owners specifically asked for peanut brittle. "When in doubt, just say yes" is a longstanding business slogan of ours, so with the gauntlet thrown down, we set out to make a peanut brittle worthy of a Canadian icon. The rest is history, and we launched it in over a hundred Roots locations that Christmas. The best part is that we fell in love with the product ourselves. It has all the caramel flavour of a toffee, but with the higher nut and lower butter content, it somehow seems a little friendlier on the waistline.

2 cups + 2 tablespoons granulated sugar

1 cup corn syrup

½ cup water

1 pound blanched unsalted unroasted peanuts

2 tablespoons unsalted butter

1½ teaspoons pure vanilla extract

1½ teaspoons baking soda

1 teaspoon salt

Tip

There is no need to use roasted nuts, as the intense heat from the sugar will cook them perfectly.

1. Line a baking sheet with parchment paper.

2. In a medium saucepan over medium heat, combine the sugar, corn syrup and water. Bring to a boil, stirring constantly, then cover and boil for 2 minutes, without stirring.

3. Remove the lid and continue to cook, without stirring, until a candy thermometer reads 240°F. Stir in the peanuts and continue to cook, stirring constantly, until the thermometer reads 320°F and the toffee is a light golden colour. Remove from the heat and stir in the butter, vanilla, baking soda and salt.

4. Immediately pour the brittle onto the lined baking sheet and spread it with a rubber spatula until it fills most of the tray. Allow the toffee to cool completely before breaking it into pieces. The brittle can be stored in an airtight container at room temperature for up to 8 weeks.

Recipe is naturally gluten-free.

Photo on page 195.

DECORATIVE CAKE TRUFFLES

Decorative cake pops and truffles were created by bakeries to make use of leftover cake, and they quickly became a popular treat. They are essentially a delicious combination of cake and buttercream, hand rolled into balls and dipped in chocolate. Freeze any leftover cake or cupcakes you might have until you have enough to make these truffles. Or, if you're like most people and the phrase "leftover cake and cupcakes" is an oxymoron, simply bake a small batch of cake to use in this recipe.

Classic Vanilla Layer Cake (prepare ½ batch, page 82, using a 9-inch square cake pan or two 9-inch round cake pans, but reduce the baking time slightly for the thinner cakes)

3 tablespoons Classic Vanilla Buttercream (page 222 or use store-bought icing), room temperature

3 to 4 cups white chocolate coating discs

Tip

Both the cake balls and the coating chocolate should be close to room temperature, otherwise the difference in temperature will cause the chocolate to crack as it sets.

While vanilla cake is easiest because it generally has more structure, you can use other types of cake and adjust the quantity of buttercream accordingly. If you are using a richly pigmented cake like red velvet or chocolate, you may need to double dip in the coating chocolate.

1. In a medium bowl, crumble the cake into fine crumbs. Stir in the buttercream a tablespoon at a time until the cake forms a dough that will hold a ball shape.

2. Spoon out even portions of the dough and roll each one between your hands until it forms a 1½-inch ball. The more even the ball is at this stage, the more uniform the cake truffles will be once dipped. Place the balls on a baking sheet and set aside.

3. Melt the chocolate discs in a medium bowl in the microwave, in 30-second intervals on medium power so the chocolate doesn't burn, stirring after each interval until melted and smooth. If you would like to colour your cake pops, add melted pre-coloured coating chocolate to the melted white chocolate. Do not use food colouring, which will cause the chocolate to seize.

4. Line a second baking sheet with parchment paper. To coat the truffles, place a cake ball on the tines of a fork and gently lower it into the melted chocolate until it is completely covered. Lift it out and allow the excess chocolate to drip back into the bowl for 20 to 30 seconds. (Dipping cake pops can be a lengthy process, but allowing the time for excess chocolate to drip off will ensure a much more attractive final result.) Gently transfer the cake ball off the fork—easing it off with a skewer helps—and onto the baking sheet. You can decorate with sprinkles now, while the chocolate is wet, or after the chocolate has set (see step 5). Repeat to fully coat all the truffles. Set aside until the chocolate has fully set.

5. As an additional decorative option, you can melt some coloured chocolate and drizzle it over the tops of the fully set cake truffles. Have fun and get creative. You can also sprinkle with coloured jimmies or edible glitter that will stick to the drizzle.

6. Place each cake truffle inside a small candy cup or mini cupcake liner. The truffles can be stored in an airtight container at room temperature for up to 4 days. The chocolate coating seals in the cake and keeps it fresh.

1. You will need a foam block and about 35 sucker sticks. Follow steps 1 through 3 on page 197.

2. Once all the balls and the chocolate are ready, dip the end of a sucker stick into the melted chocolate and then insert it about halfway into the cake ball. Repeat with all the balls. The chocolate will help the stick to stay firmly in place as you dip.

3. Holding a cake pop by the stick, dip the whole ball and about $1/2$-inch of the stick into the chocolate. It is important to cover some of the stick or the stick will move through the top of the cake pop as it dries. Lift out the cake pop and hold it upside down for 20 to 30 seconds so any excess chocolate can drip off. Turn the cake pop upright and stick it into the foam block. Repeat to fully coat all the cake pops.

4. You can decorate with sprinkles while the chocolate is wet, or melt some coloured chocolate and drizzle it over the tops of the fully set cake pops. Have fun and get creative. You can also sprinkle with coloured jimmies or edible glitter that will stick to the drizzle.

FRENCH MERINGUE KISSES

Meringue kisses are so simple to make yet so delicate and pretty that it almost seems too good to be true. In fact, we started making them as a decorative item to fill apothecary jars on sweet tables and to add some colour around the shop. It wasn't until we noticed the jars slowly emptying that we realized people were desperate to eat them. We started packaging up seasonal colours for purchase, and they flew off the shelves. How could something so simple conjure such an impassioned response? We think it's the full-frontal assault of sweetness paired with the perfect balance of crunchy and chewy texture.

7 large egg whites

1¾ cups granulated sugar

Food colouring and/or flavour extract, if desired

Tip

To make these kisses your own, whip a few drops of food colouring and/or flavour extracts into the beaten meringue, and add garnishes like sprinkles before baking.

1. Preheat the oven to 250°F. Line 2 baking sheets with parchment paper.

2. In a medium saucepan, heat an inch or so of water until barely simmering.

3. In a medium heatproof bowl, whisk together the egg whites and sugar. Place the bowl over the barely simmering water and heat, continuously but gently stirring, until the sugar has dissolved. Transfer the egg whites to the bowl of a stand mixer fitted with the whisk attachment. Whisk on medium speed until the meringue is cool to the touch, tripled in volume and holds stiff peaks, 8 to 10 minutes.

4. Fit a piping bag with a $^3/_8$-inch star tip and fill with meringue. Pipe 2-inch kisses, about $^1/_2$-inch apart, onto the lined baking sheets.

5. Bake for 2 to 3 hours, until the meringues are firm to the touch but still have a soft centre. They should remain white. Allow the meringues to cool completely on the baking sheets on a wire rack. The meringues can be stored in an airtight container at room temperature for up to 1 month.

   Recipe is naturally gluten-free.

   Recipe is naturally dairy-free.

Fleur de Sel CARAMEL CORN

At the shop we simply refer to this as "crack corn" and we all know that if you break the seal and have even one piece, it's all over. While we don't offer any rehab if you give in, we do offer solidarity. Our very own accountant informed us that our small bag fits perfectly in his car cup holder, where he proceeds to grab handfuls on the way home from work and has, on more than one occasion, cursed us as he polishes off another bag. We created our crack corn after a work trip to New York, where we stumbled upon an entire wall of gourmet caramel corn in Dean & DeLuca. After trying several varieties, we knew exactly the things we liked and things we would change. We went to work as soon as we got home, and we hope you'll have as much fun making this as we did.

---

1 cup unsalted butter

1 cup loosely packed brown sugar

⅓ cup corn syrup

1 teaspoon pure vanilla extract

1 teaspoon fleur de sel

Rounded ¼ teaspoon baking soda

15 cups popped corn (from ⅔ cup popcorn kernels)

Tip

Turn the caramel corn into a fun trail mix by adding ½ cup of pretzel pieces or nuts (or a combination of both) at the same time the popped corn is stirred into the hot caramel mixture. You can also drizzle melted chocolate over the cooled caramel corn.

1. Preheat the oven to 275°F. Line 2 baking sheets with parchment paper.

2. In a large stockpot over medium-high heat, combine the butter, brown sugar, corn syrup and vanilla. Once the butter has melted, cover and cook, without stirring, until the mixture is a light caramel colour, about 5 minutes.

3. Remove the lid and stir in the baking soda and fleur de sel and baking soda. Add the popped corn and stir with a large spoon until the popcorn is fully coated. Spread the popcorn onto the lined baking sheets.

4. Bake for 1 hour. Remove from the oven and immediately stir the popcorn with a wooden spoon to break apart any large chunks and to evenly distribute the caramel. Allow the caramel corn to cool completely before serving. The caramel corn can be stored in an airtight container at room temperature for up to 3 weeks.

Recipe is naturally gluten-free.

HOT CHOCOLATE
with Toasted Vanilla Marshmallows

When we first opened our shop we were asked to participate in a local fall street festival. We decided to make homemade hot chocolate and toast our signature marshmallows à la minute in front of customers. We soon found ourselves, in chocolate-covered chef whites, industrial blowtorches in hand, torching ten marshmallows at a time while portioning scalding cups of cocoa in front of a never-ending lineup, in a manner that could only be described as a third-degree burn waiting to happen. As it turns out, all that stress and neglect of fire code was worth it, as it ended up inspiring our number one drink.

VANILLA MARSHMALLOWS

3 tablespoons unflavoured gelatin (3 envelopes)

1¼ cups water

1½ cups granulated sugar

¾ cup corn syrup

¼ teaspoon salt

1 tablespoon pure vanilla extract

1 cup cornstarch

1 cup icing sugar, sifted

HOT CHOCOLATE

1¼ cups finely chopped semisweet chocolate (7 ounces)

½ cup cocoa powder

½ cup granulated sugar

5¼ cups whole milk

Tip

At our shops many of our customers love to mix half hot chocolate with half espresso. Try this at home to shake up your morning java routine.

1. Line 2 baking sheets with parchment paper and lightly spray with non-stick cooking spray.

2. To make the vanilla marshmallows, in a small bowl, sprinkle the gelatin over ¼ cup of the water. Let stand until all the water is absorbed by the gelatin and a firm, rubbery mass forms. Set aside.

3. In a medium saucepan, combine the remaining 1 cup of water, the sugar, corn syrup and salt. Heat over medium-high heat, stirring, until hot to the touch and the sugar has dissolved. Remove from the heat and whisk in the bloomed gelatin and vanilla until fully incorporated.

4. Transfer the mixture to the bowl of a stand mixer fitted with the whisk attachment and whisk on high speed until the mixture has cooled, doubled in size and holds soft peaks, about 10 minutes. The marshmallow mass should be light and airy and be able to hold its shape when piped.

5. Transfer the mixture to a piping bag fitted with a 1-inch round tip and pipe 2-inch kisses onto the lined baking sheets.

6. In a bowl, whisk together the cornstarch and icing sugar. Using a fine-mesh sieve, lightly dust the tops of the piped marshmallows with some of the cornstarch mixture. Leave the marshmallows to dry overnight, uncovered at room temperature. Put the remaining cornstarch mixture in a bowl and set aside.

7. The next day, line a baking sheet with parchment paper. Add a few marshmallows at a time to the bowl of cornstarch mixture and gently toss to fully coat. Take care not to allow the marshmallows to stick together when coating. Remove from the bowl and place on the lined baking sheet.

8. In a fine-mesh sieve, gently shake a few marshmallows at a time to get rid of any excess cornstarch mixture. Transfer the marshmallows to an airtight container. The marshmallows can be stored at room temperature for up to 3 weeks.

9. To make the hot chocolate, place the chopped chocolate in a medium heatproof bowl and set aside.

10. In a medium saucepan, whisk together the cocoa powder and sugar. Add the milk and whisk to combine. Bring just to a simmer. Do not boil. Slowly pour the hot milk over the chopped chocolate, whisking constantly until the chocolate is melted and smooth. Strain the hot chocolate through a fine-mesh sieve into a large measuring cup for easy portioning.

11. To toast the marshmallows, place a few marshmallows on a baking sheet and using a kitchen blowtorch, toast each marshmallows until golden. Pour hot chocolate into mugs, top with marshmallows and serve immediately.

Recipe is naturally gluten-free.

Vanilla Marshmallow recipe is naturally dairy-free.

DOUBLE CHOCOLATE MARSHMALLOWS

In France, handmade guimauves (marshmallows) are a favourite confection that can be found in almost every confiserie (sweet shop). Piped kisses, giggling squares and long, twisted ropes are among a wide range of shapes. Of course, marshmallows are a popular treat in North America as well, but this is where the similarity ends. Unfortunately our highly processed, artificially flavoured puffs of sugar have nothing like the texture and taste of the homemade version. When made from scratch, marshmallows are naturally flavoured with extracts, fruit purées or high-quality cocoa, and the texture is light and smooth as velvet. Our double chocolate marshmallows are particularly tempting and eat less like a garnish and more like a treat unto themselves.

3 tablespoons unflavoured gelatin (3 envelopes)

1½ cups water

1½ cups granulated sugar

¾ cup corn syrup

4½ teaspoons cocoa powder

¼ teaspoon salt

1 tablespoon pure vanilla extract

1 cup cocoa powder, for coating

Recipe is naturally gluten-free.

Recipe is naturally dairy-free.

Tip

A good-quality dark cocoa powder makes all the difference in the world when it comes to flavour.

1. Line 2 baking sheets with parchment paper and lightly spray with non-stick cooking spray.

2. In a small bowl, sprinkle the gelatin over ¼ cup of the water. Let stand until all the water is absorbed by the gelatin and a firm, rubbery mass forms. Set aside.

3. In a medium saucepan, combine the remaining 1¼ cups of water, the sugar, corn syrup, 4½ teaspoons cocoa and salt. Heat over medium-high heat, stirring, until hot to the touch and the sugar has dissolved. Remove from the heat and whisk in the bloomed gelatin and the vanilla until fully incorporated.

4. Transfer the mixture to the bowl of a stand mixer fitted with the whisk attachment and whisk on high speed until the mixture has cooled, doubled in volume and holds soft peaks, about 10 minutes. The marshmallow mass should also be light and airy and be able to hold its shape when piped.

5. Transfer the mixture to a piping bag fitted with a 1-inch round tip and pipe forty 2-inch kisses onto each lined baking sheet. Using a fine-mesh sieve, lightly dust the tops of the piped marshmallows with some of the 1 cup cocoa powder. Leave the marshmallows to dry overnight, uncovered and at room temperature. Put the remaining cocoa powder in a bowl and set aside.

6. The next day, line a baking sheet with parchment paper. Add a few marshmallows at a time to the bowl of cocoa powder and gently toss to fully coat. Take care not to allow the marshmallows to stick together when coating. Remove from the bowl and place on the lined baking sheet.

7. In a fine-mesh sieve, gently shake a few marshmallows at a time to get rid of any excess cocoa. Transfer the marshmallows to an airtight container. The marshmallows can be stored at room temperature for up to 3 weeks.

LEMONADE

It's funny, when you're in the baking business you become aware of all sorts of things you never noticed before. Particularly with regards to flavour. Growing up, we thought nothing of the bright little lemon-shaped bottle of "real" lemon juice in the fridge, or our summers filled with Country Time, but once you have lemon curd made with freshly squeezed lemons, there's no going back. The same goes for lemonade. There really is no substitute for the real deal. This is a simple, quick recipe that you can enhance with some additions like watermelon or raspberry.

1 cup granulated sugar

8 cups water

2 cups freshly squeezed lemon juice (from about 10 lemons)

Add one of the following variations (optional):

¼ cup dried lavender flowers

½ small watermelon, peeled and puréed, plus small chopped watermelon pieces for garnish

¼ cup Raspberry Purée (prepare ½ batch, page 245), plus fresh raspberries for garnish

1 small bunch fresh mint leaves

Tip

If you are adding the fresh mint, break up the leaves before adding to release their natural oils and impart more flavour in the lemonade. Strain out the mint leaves before storing leftover lemonade, or they will turn black as they age.

1. In small saucepan, bring the sugar and 1 cup of the water to a boil. Continue to boil until the sugar has fully dissolved.

2. Pour the syrup into a container and place in the fridge to cool completely. If you are adding lavender, add it at this stage. (Using a loose-leaf tea bag or tea ball makes removing the lavender easier.)

3. Once the syrup has chilled, add the lemon juice and 7 cups of water. Stir to combine.

    • *If you added lavender,* strain the lemonade or remove the tea bag.

    • *If you are adding watermelon or raspberry purée,* add it at this stage.

    • *If you are adding fresh mint,* break up the leaves and add to the lemonade.

4. Serve chilled and over ice. The lemonade will keep in the fridge for up to 3 days.

    Recipe is naturally gluten-free.

    Recipe is naturally dairy-free.

"Make It Your Own"
GRANOLA

Granola is delicious and versatile. It works equally well as a breakfast cereal, a topping for yogurt or a quick snack. Unfortunately, gourmet varieties are often quite expensive and there are limited flavour selections. Granola is very easy to make at home, and we wanted to create a recipe that would have a tasty base that could be enhanced with all kinds of additions. We have listed a few of our favourites, but you can jazz it up any way you like.

GRANOLA

⅓ cup unsalted butter, melted

1½ teaspoons pure vanilla extract

¼ teaspoon salt

4 cups large-flake rolled oats

⅓ cup loosely packed brown sugar

2 teaspoons cinnamon

½ cup maple syrup

Add one of the following variations:

CHOCOLATE, HAZELNUT, BANANA AND COCONUT

½ cup dark chocolate chips

½ cup hazelnuts, coarsely chopped

½ cup banana chips, coarsely chopped

½ cup flaked coconut

ALMOND, APRICOT AND CRANBERRY

½ cup almonds, coarsely chopped

½ cup dried apricots, chopped into small pieces

½ cup dried cranberries

1. Preheat the oven to 300°F. Line a baking sheet with parchment paper.

2. In a small bowl, combine the melted butter, vanilla and salt.

3. In a large bowl, combine the oats, brown sugar, cinnamon and maple syrup. Add the coconut or nuts from your chosen variation.

4. Drizzle the melted butter mixture over the oat mixture and stir to fully combine all the ingredients. Spread the granola on the lined baking sheet.

5. Bake for 30 to 35 minutes, stirring with a spatula a few times, until the oats are lightly golden. Remove from the oven. Add the dried fruits or banana chips from your chosen variation now, and stir to combine. Allow the granola to cool completely on the baking sheet. Add the chocolate chips from your chosen variation to the fully cooled granola.

6. The granola can be stored in an airtight container at room temperature for up to 3 weeks.

   Recipe is naturally gluten-free.

 Tip This recipe is very forgiving, so get creative by adding nut butters or additional spices before baking.

9

BUTTERCREAMS
FROSTINGS
AND FILLINGS

FILLING, MASKING AND CAKE ASSEMBLY

Our layer cakes are one of our signature desserts at Bobbette & Belle, and we are known for level cakes with even layers and expertly applied buttercream. Filling and masking a layer cake is one of those tasks that benefits most from repeated practice, but here are some tips and instructions you can follow to help make the process easier and to help achieve an irresistible cake.

We recommend using a thin cake board the same diameter as the cake you are filling so that it does not show when you transfer the finished cake to a cake stand or serving plate. To ensure the cake board does not shift while the cake is being masked, at the shops we put a small non-slip grip pad under the board, but you can also tape the underside of the cake board to the turntable.

1. The first step is to cut off any dome on the top to make an even layer of cake. Once you have chilled your cake layers to make them firmer, place one layer on a cutting board. Place the edge of a long serrated knife on the outer top edge of the cake and cut off the dome, leaving a flat surface. Repeat the process for the other two layers.

2. Place a dab of buttercream or frosting on your cake board to hold the cake in place as you work, then lay the first layer on top, trimmed side up. Spoon a large dollop of your filling in the centre of the cake layer. Using a large offset spatula, start moving the filling gently back and forth with light pressure while you simultaneously turn the cake stand. You will begin to see the filling evenly spread out toward the edge of the cake layer. This takes coordination and practice, but it is the easiest way to ensure an even filling that covers the whole surface of the layer without getting crumbs in it. The finished layer of filling should be $1/4$- to $1/3$-inch thick.

   NOTE: If you are filling with a curd, fill a pastry bag fitted with a round tip with classic vanilla buttercream (page 222). Pipe the buttercream around the outer edge of the cake layers to create a "dam" for the curd. Spoon the curd directly onto the cake layer and spread outward until it meets the edge of the dam.

3. Place the next cake layer on top, this time cut side down. This will allow you to spread your filling on a smooth, uncut surface. (You do not do this with the bottom layer because you need the stability of the uncut side on the bottom.) Smooth the filling over this layer just as you did with the first.

4. Place the final cake layer on top, cut side down. You will be able to see already how even your cake is, with straight sides and a level top. Now you have a few options. Most of our cakes are masked on the outside with buttercream for a smooth finish. We will describe that technique here. If you would prefer to create a swirl or a rustic finish, see the variations on page 217. Buttercream works for any finish, while frostings tend to look best in a rustic finish, as they are difficult to smooth out without dragging.

5. To reduce the risk of crumbs working their way through the icing, give the whole outside of the cake a "crumb coat." Using your offset spatula, apply a very thin see-through layer of buttercream over the entire top and sides of the cake. Chill the cake on the cake stand in the fridge for 30 minutes to allow the filling and the crumb coat to set.

6. Remove the cake from the fridge. Place a large mound of buttercream on the top of the cake and use the same technique you used to spread the filling, but this time allow the buttercream to extend about $1/2$-inch beyond the edge of the cake. Hold the blade of your offset spatula on a slight angle over the top of the cake and rotate the cake stand to smooth out the top.

7. Now use your offset spatula to apply lots of buttercream all around the sides of the cake. You are not doing any smoothing at this point—you are simply covering the cake in plenty of buttercream. Make sure the side buttercream meets up with the overhanging buttercream on top.

8. Now it's time for the fun part. Place your bench scraper at a 90-degree angle with the blade barely touching the cake and the edge resting tightly against the cake stand. Angle the bench scraper toward you and begin turning the cake stand. Don't apply too much pressure at the beginning. You will begin to collect extra buttercream on your scraper while seeing the buttercream smooth out. Once you are used to the feeling, increase the pressure and speed. Believe it or not, speed is your friend when it comes to creating a smooth buttercream finish. Every once in a while, clean the excess buttercream off your bench scraper and keep going. Be careful not to remove too much buttercream from the sides or you will start to see cake underneath. If this accidentally happens, just apply more buttercream and continue the process.

9. You will notice a small wall of buttercream start to form at the top edge of the cake as the smoothing of the sides pushes buttercream upward. Use the edge of your offset spatula to push the excess buttercream toward the centre of the top. If there is quite a bit of excess buttercream, use a slight sweeping motion as you do this in order to lift off any excess as you go. Clean the excess off your spatula before

continuing. This is how we achieve such a sharp edge at the top of our cakes. It takes a bit of practice but is an oddly satisfying part of the process. It is fun to see such a clean edge appear as you work your way around the cake.

10. Once the cake is fully masked in smooth buttercream, you can add any additional toppings the recipe calls for. We love the look of dripping chocolate glaze or caramel. For both of these, allow the cake to set in the fridge for 15 minutes. You want it set but not too cold or the topping will "seize" when it comes in contact with the icing. Apply the topping to the centre of the top of the cake. It will spread a bit by itself, but to get it to spill nicely over the sides, use the same offset spatula technique you used to spread the filling, only this time use a very light touch as you slowly rotate the cake stand. The goal is to gently push some of the topping uniformly over the top edge of the cake so it will run down the sides. You have to work gently but fairly quickly before the topping sets. Once finished, garnish with any additional toppings and voilà, you're done. Now you can dig in!

THE SIGNATURE SWIRL (A)

Once you have completed step 7, continue with steps 8 and 9, but this time don't worry about trying to get a perfectly smooth finish. Once the entire outside of the cake is fairly smooth, place the tip of your offset spatula at a slight angle touching the bottom edge of the cake. You can use a large or small offset spatula, whichever you find easier. Begin rotating the cake stand fairly quickly, and with each full rotation move the tip of the spatula upward without taking it off the cake. This fluid motion will create one continuous swirl. It will take some practice to find the right pressure. Keep the cake stand moving fairly quickly or you will see "hesitation" marks. If you want to practise, you can always apply a little more buttercream, smooth it out quickly with the bench scraper and give it another whirl.

A RUSTIC FINISH (B)

This is the simplest way to finish a cake, but it is no less dramatic. Nothing gives the deliciously tempting look of home baking more than a rustic finish. In fact, if you don't have time to make all the toppings and garnishes for one of our cakes, you can simply complete the cake with a rustic finish of buttercream or frosting.

Mask your cake up to the end of step 5. Apply your frosting or buttercream with the back of a large dessert spoon. The spoon will naturally create a rustic appearance, but you can enhance this by flicking the spoon as you finish applying some icing or by applying less or more pressure as you go.

A few recipes in this book call for finishes that are a bit more decorative than usual: the flower piping technique (used on the Tart Raspberry Lemon Cakes, page 98, and the Decorative Sugar Cookies, page 42), the rose piping technique (on the Piped Rose Lemon Cupcakes, page 62) and the white piping decoration (on the Holiday Gingerbread House Cookies, page 48). These decorative techniques are the first ones we learned when we started making our cakes. After teaching many a beginner and advanced piping class, it always comes as a surprise how nervous people get about piping. It's true that it can seem daunting at first, but rest assured, once you get going it is an incredibly enjoyable and relaxing task. The following techniques may be used (as shown) or piped directly onto sugar cookies, mini cakes and cupcakes.

The key thing to remember is that the piping bag is one with your feelings. That sounds nuts, but trust us: if you feel nervous or judge yourself too harshly as you go along, your piping will reveal your hesitation and anxiety. We recommend piping on parchment or your countertop first. Pencil words and pictures on the parchment and try to pipe over the lines. Pipe until you find your sweet spot, the most comfortable bag and tip position for you and the best pressure. For those of you who are particularly crafty or creative, this type of fine motor task may come easily, but if you tend to think of yourself as not particularly artistic, remember that piping is a lot like writing, and once you get a feel for your "writing" utensil, it will begin to feel natural.

GINGERBREAD HOUSE PIPING

You will need a small round tip (#2 or #3).

1. Give your white royal icing a mix on the stand mixer before filling your bag. This will help to reduce air bubbles and give it a better texture for piping.

2. Fit your piping bag with a coupler and the small round tip and fill the bag half to two-thirds full with royal icing. Secure the end tightly with an elastic. If you need to practise, draw some houses on parchment and pipe them before moving on to your cookies.

3. Always angle your piping bag away from the piping, much the way you hold a pen. When piping straight edges, it is often easiest to hold the piping tip an inch or two above the cookies and let the icing "fall" into a line. This is also true for curves, but you will need to hold the tip a bit closer.

4. If you like, sprinkle some edible glitter or coarse sugar onto the icing to make it even more snowy looking. Be sure to apply it as you go, because the glitter will roll off if the royal icing has set.

5. Allow the houses to dry at room temperature for 12 hours before layering them for storage.

PIPING FIVE-PETAL FLOWERS AND ROSES

When piping decorative flowers, fill your piping bag only half to two-thirds full and secure the end tightly with an elastic. Hold the bag near the elastic. It is always best to apply pressure from the top rather than right by the tip. (Think of a tube of toothpaste.) As you use your icing, you will periodically need to tighten your bag. Remove the elastic, twist the bag tighter, then reapply the elastic. The internal pressure from the tight elastic improves piping and helps prevent your hand from cramping. Instructions follow on page 220–221.

FIVE-PETAL FLOWERS

You will need a petal tip (a #104 or #105 will be perfect), a very small round tip, a coupler and a flower nail (as shown). A petal tip is wider at one end than the other which allows us to mimic the look of different types of petals.

1. Cut out a bunch of 1½-inch parchment squares. The more you cut, the more practice you'll have. Draw a circle on each one and divide the "pie" into five even pieces. These will be your petal guides.

2. Fit your piping bag with the coupler and the petal tip and fill the bag half to two-thirds full with buttercream or royal icing. Secure the end tightly with an elastic. Dab a little icing on the centre of the top of the flower nail and press a parchment square, pencil side down, onto it to hold it in place.

3. Hold the flower nail in your non-dominant hand and the piping bag in your dominant hand, holding the bag near the elastic. Place the wider end of the piping tip on the centre of the parchment square. To shape the first petal, begin to apply pressure on the piping bag and pipe away from you as you rotate the flower nail counter-clockwise and the piping bag clockwise. As the tip approaches the pencil mark indicating the end of that petal, bring the thin side of the tip quickly toward the centre, then stop applying pressure. This will form the end of the petal and cause the icing to break off.

4. Repeat for the remaining four petals.

5. Switch out the petal tip for a very small round tip and pipe a series of dots in the centre of the flower to finish it off. Remove the flower—still on its parchment—from the flower nail and place it on a baking sheet. Royal icing flowers will need to dry for at least 12 hours before you can remove them from the parchment. Chill buttercream flowers in the fridge for at least 30 minutes (the colder they are, the less likely they are to break) before removing them from the parchment and applying to the cake or cupcakes.

PIPED ROSES

You will need a large round tip (a #7 or #8), a petal tip (#105 is best) and a coupler.

1. Have your mini cupcakes waiting on a tray. Fit your piping bag with the coupler and the large round tip and fill the bag half to two-thirds full with buttercream or royal icing. Secure the end tightly with an elastic. Pipe a "kiss" of buttercream about ¾-inch tall on the top of each cupcake, then place the entire tray in the fridge to chill. The "kiss" will act as the bud for your roses. Many petals will be piped on top of the bud, so it is best to allow it to chill and harden.

2. Switch out the round tip for the petal tip. Hold a cupcake in your non-dominant hand, and the piping bag in your dominant hand, holding the bag near the elastic. Now, picture making a series of rainbows. The wide part of the tip will form the inside of the rainbow and the thin part of the tip will make the top of the rainbow as you pipe.

3. Start by piping three slightly overlapping rainbows that cover the "kiss" or bud, rotating the cupcake as you pipe and tilting your tip toward the bud.

4. Begin your second layer of rainbows, this time starting in the centre of a previous petal. The goal is to overlap the petals in a natural-looking offset fashion. As you pipe each layer of petals, you will need to increase the number of petals while also changing the tilt of your piping bag slowly from toward the bud to away from the bud. This will give the effect of the rose opening. Pipe petals almost to the edge of the cupcake.

5. Repeat for all the cupcakes, switching colours if you like to create more of a garden feel.

CLASSIC VANILLA BUTTERCREAM

**MAKES ENOUGH TO FROST 12 TO 15 CUPCAKES;
DOUBLE THE RECIPE TO FILL AND MASK A 9-INCH ROUND THREE-LAYER CAKE**

We use this classic Swiss meringue buttercream as the base for most of our buttercream recipes. The method is simple and results in a stable buttercream that is excellent for piping and for filling cakes. It can also be applied in a perfectly smooth fashion that is not possible with other frostings.

4 large egg whites (½ cup)

1 cup granulated sugar

1 pound unsalted butter, cut into 1-inch cubes, room temperature

1 teaspoon pure vanilla extract

Tip

Because the feature flavour in this buttercream is vanilla, use a high-quality pure vanilla extract such as Nielsen-Massey Madagascar Bourbon Vanilla (see source guide, page 248).

Swiss meringue buttercream is always best served at room temperature to retain its light, fluffy texture. Because of its high butter content, it becomes quite stiff when refrigerated, so allow any chilled dessert with buttercream a good amount of time to sit at room temperature before serving.

1. In a medium saucepan, bring an inch or so of water to a simmer.

2. In a large heatproof bowl, combine the egg whites and sugar. Place over the simmering water and whisk gently until very hot to the touch or a candy thermometer reads 140°F. Immediately pour the egg white mixture into the bowl of a stand mixer fitted with the whisk attachment.

3. Whisk on medium-high speed until the egg whites have cooled to room temperature, doubled in volume and hold medium peaks, 8 to 10 minutes.

4. Turn the mixer to medium-low speed and slowly add the butter a few cubes at a time, increasing the speed to medium-high after each addition and beating until the butter is fully incorporated before adding more. Once all the butter has been added, continue to beat on medium-high until the buttercream is light and fluffy, 1 to 2 minutes. Stop the mixer to scrape down the sides of the bowl, making sure to scrape the bottom as well. Add the vanilla and beat on medium speed for 2 more minutes.

5. Use immediately or store in an airtight container in the fridge for up to 1 week. Bring buttercream to room temperature before using. Any leftovers may be frozen for up to 3 months.

Recipe is naturally gluten-free.

CHOCOLATE BUTTERCREAM

**MAKES ENOUGH TO FROST 12 TO 15 CUPCAKES;
DOUBLE THE RECIPE TO FILL AND MASK A 9-INCH ROUND THREE-LAYER CAKE**

This is a classic Swiss meringue buttercream with chocolate added. For the best flavor, we recommend using a high-quality chocolate such as Lindt or Valrhona. Chocolate buttercream is a great option if you would like a slightly less chocolaty and less sweet option that a chocolate frosting.

4 large egg whites (½ cup)

1 cup granulated sugar

1 pound unsalted butter, cut into 1-inch cubes, room temperature

1 teaspoon pure vanilla extract

1 cup chopped 70% to 85% dark chocolate (6 ounces), melted and cooled to just above room temperature

Tip

The percentage of cocoa in the chocolate has a profound effect on its flavour. If you like a lighter chocolate taste, look for a 65% cocoa content. If you prefer a rich, dark chocolate flavour, look for 85% cocoa or higher.

1. In a medium saucepan, bring an inch or so of water to a simmer.

2. In a large heatproof bowl, combine the egg whites and sugar. Place over the simmering water and whisk gently until very hot to the touch or a candy thermometer reads 140°F. Immediately pour the egg white mixture into the bowl of a stand mixer fitted with the whisk attachment.

3. Whisk on medium-high speed until the egg whites have cooled to room temperature, doubled in volume and hold medium peaks, 8 to 10 minutes.

4. Turn the mixer to medium-low speed and slowly add the butter a few cubes at a time, increasing the speed to medium-high after each addition and beating until the butter is fully incorporated before adding more. Once all the butter has been added, continue to beat on medium-high until the buttercream is light and fluffy, 1 to 2 minutes. Stop the mixer to scrape down the sides of the bowl, making sure to scrape the bottom as well. Add the vanilla and beat on medium speed for 2 more minutes.

5. With the mixer on medium speed, add the melted chocolate in a slow stream, beating until fully combined. Stop to scrape down the sides of the bowl, then beat for an additional minute.

6. Use immediately or store in an airtight container in the fridge for up to 1 week. Bring buttercream to room temperature before using. Any leftovers may be frozen for up to 3 months.

Recipe is naturally gluten-free.

CHOCOLATE HAZELNUT BUTTERCREAM

**MAKES ENOUGH TO FROST 12 TO 15 CUPCAKES;
DOUBLE THE RECIPE TO FILL AND MASK A 9-INCH ROUND THREE-LAYER CAKE**

This delicious flavouring for classic buttercream is reminiscent of the inside of a Ferrero Rocher, and it is worth sourcing a high-quality gianduja chocolate. It is quite a soft chocolate, so you may need to keep your cake or cupcakes chilled to retain stability over time. You can also add a bit of melted dark chocolate to tighten up the buttercream.

4 large egg whites (½ cup)

1 cup granulated sugar

1 pound unsalted butter, cut into 1-inch cubes, room temperature

1 teaspoon pure vanilla extract

1 cup chopped gianduja (hazelnut chocolate) (5 ounces), melted and cooled to just above room temperature

Tip

Depending on where you buy your chocolate, gianduja may be sold by that name or simply called hazelnut chocolate. It is readily available in most specialty food stores or online. Gianduja is a blend of chocolate and hazelnut paste. Do not confuse it with chocolate with hazelnut pieces.

1. In a medium saucepan, bring an inch or so of water to a simmer.

2. In a large heatproof bowl, combine the egg whites and sugar. Place over the simmering water and whisk gently until very hot to the touch or a candy thermometer reads 140°F. Immediately pour the egg white mixture into the bowl of a stand mixer fitted with the whisk attachment.

3. Whisk on medium-high speed until the egg whites have cooled to room temperature, doubled in volume and hold medium peaks, 8 to 10 minutes.

4. Turn the mixer to medium-low speed and slowly add the butter a few cubes at a time, increasing the speed to medium-high after each addition and beating until the butter is fully incorporated before adding more. Once all the butter has been added, continue to beat on medium-high until the buttercream is light and fluffy, 1 to 2 minutes. Stop the mixer to scrape down the sides of the bowl, making sure to scrape the bottom as well. Add the vanilla and beat on medium speed for 2 more minutes.

5. With the mixer on medium speed, add the melted chocolate in a slow stream, beating until fully combined. Stop to scrape down the sides of the bowl, then beat for an additional minute.

6. Use immediately or store in an airtight container in the fridge for up to 1 week. Bring buttercream to room temperature before using. Any leftovers may be frozen for up to 3 months.

**MAKES ENOUGH TO FROST 12 TO 15 CUPCAKES;
DOUBLE THE RECIPE TO FILL AND MASK A 9-INCH ROUND THREE-LAYER CAKE**

It may seem time consuming to make caramel sauce from scratch, but it is well worth the effort in this recipe. The deep caramel flavours the buttercream in a way that a store-bought brand couldn't. As a bonus, the sauce recipe makes more than is required for the buttercream, so you can use the extra as a garnish to add even more caramel flavour.

4 large egg whites (½ cup)

1 cup granulated sugar

1 pound unsalted butter, cut into 1-inch cubes, room temperature

1 teaspoon pure vanilla extract

¼ cup Salted Caramel Sauce (page 190)

Tip

You may be tempted to add more caramel sauce to the buttercream, but don't. Too much will affect the stability and make it difficult to pipe or mask with. Instead, use the extra caramel sauce as a garnish on top.

1. In a medium saucepan, bring an inch or so of water to a simmer.

2. In a large heatproof bowl, combine the egg whites and sugar. Place over the simmering water and whisk gently until very hot to the touch or a candy thermometer reads 140°F. Immediately pour the egg white mixture into the bowl of a stand mixer fitted with the whisk attachment.

3. Whisk on medium-high speed until the egg whites have cooled to room temperature, doubled in volume and hold medium peaks, 8 to 10 minutes.

4. Turn the mixer to medium-low speed and slowly add the butter a few cubes at a time, increasing the speed to medium-high after each addition and beating until the butter is fully incorporated before adding more. Once all the butter has been added, continue to beat on medium-high until the buttercream is light and fluffy, 1 to 2 minutes. Stop the mixer to scrape down the sides of the bowl, making sure to scrape the bottom as well. Add the vanilla and beat on medium speed for 2 more minutes.

5. With the mixer on medium speed, add the salted caramel sauce in a slow stream until fully combined. Stop to scrape down the sides of the bowl, then beat for 2 more minutes.

6. Use immediately or store in an airtight container in the fridge for up to 1 week. Bring buttercream to room temperature before using. Any leftovers may be frozen for up to 3 months.

   Recipe is naturally gluten-free.

BROWN SUGAR BUTTERCREAM

MAKES ENOUGH TO FROST 12 TO 15 CUPCAKES;
DOUBLE THE RECIPE TO FILL AND MASK A 9-INCH ROUND THREE-LAYER CAKE

This is very similar to vanilla buttercream, except brown sugar is used in place of white. The added flavour from the brown sugar gives the buttercream caramel notes without its actually being caramel that might upstage other flavours. The buttercream is ridiculously yummy on its own but takes well to other flavours. We add coffee extract to it to top our Caffè Latte Cupcakes (page 66), where it tastes rich and creamy but doesn't compete with the coffee flavour. Feel free to experiment with other flavours.

4 large egg whites (½ cup)

1 cup loosely packed brown sugar

1 pound unsalted butter, cut into 1-inch cubes, room temperature

2 teaspoons pure vanilla extract

Pinch of salt

Tip

Always use room-temperature butter when making Swiss meringue buttercreams. It ensures a creamy, smooth texture without off-putting clumps of butter.

1. In a medium saucepan, bring an inch or so of water to a simmer.

2. In a large heatproof bowl, combine the egg whites and brown sugar. Place over the simmering water and whisk gently until very hot to the touch or a candy thermometer reads 140°F. Immediately pour the egg white mixture into the bowl of a stand mixer fitted with the whisk attachment.

3. Whisk on medium-high speed until the egg whites have cooled to room temperature, doubled in volume and hold medium peaks, 8 to 10 minutes.

4. Turn the mixer to medium-low speed and slowly add the butter a few cubes at a time, increasing the speed to medium-high after each addition and beating until the butter is fully incorporated before adding more. Once all the butter has been added, continue to beat on medium-high until the buttercream is light and fluffy, 1 to 2 minutes. Stop the mixer to scrape down the sides of the bowl, making sure to scrape the bottom as well. Add the vanilla and a pinch of salt and beat on medium speed for 2 more minutes.

5. Use immediately or store in an airtight container in the fridge for up to 1 week. Bring buttercream to room temperature before using. Any leftovers may be frozen for up to 3 months.

Recipe is naturally gluten-free.

**MAKES ENOUGH TO FROST 12 TO 15 CUPCAKES;
DOUBLE THE RECIPE TO FILL AND MASK A 9-INCH ROUND THREE-LAYER CAKE**

Sometimes a cake wants a less sweet cream cheese buttercream rather than a sweeter cream cheese frosting. We often use this buttercream for wedding cakes, because it works best for the structure of tiered cakes and also slices cleanly.

4 large egg whites (½ cup)

1 cup granulated sugar

1 pound unsalted butter, cut into 1-inch cubes, room temperature

1 teaspoon pure vanilla extract

¼ cup cream cheese, cut into 1-inch cubes, room temperature

Tip

If the buttercream looks curdled when you add the cream cheese, simply beat on high until it becomes creamy.

1. In a medium saucepan, bring an inch or so of water to a simmer.

2. In a large heatproof bowl, combine the egg whites and sugar. Place over the simmering water and whisk gently until very hot to the touch or a candy thermometer reads 140°F. Immediately pour the egg white mixture into the bowl of a stand mixer fitted with the whisk attachment.

3. Whisk on medium-high speed until the egg whites have cooled to room temperature, doubled in volume and hold medium peaks, 8 to 10 minutes.

4. Turn the mixer to medium-low speed and slowly add the butter a few cubes at a time, increasing the speed to medium-high after each addition and beating until the butter is fully incorporated before adding more. Once all the butter has been added, continue to beat on medium-high until the buttercream is light and fluffy, 1 to 2 minutes. Stop the mixer to scrape down the sides of the bowl, making sure to scrape the bottom as well.

5. Add the vanilla and return the mixer to medium speed. Begin adding the cream cheese a cube at a time, beating until the cream cheese is fully incorporated before adding more. Once all the cream cheese has been added, increase the speed to medium-high and beat for 2 more minutes, stopping to scrape down the sides of the bowl midway.

6. Use immediately or store in an airtight container in the fridge for up to 1 week. Bring buttercream to room temperature before using. Any leftovers may be frozen for up to 3 months.

Recipe is naturally gluten-free.

RASPBERRY BUTTERCREAM

MAKES ENOUGH TO FROST 12 TO 15 CUPCAKES; DOUBLE THE RECIPE TO FILL AND MASK A 9-INCH ROUND THREE-LAYER CAKE

Raspberry buttercream is wonderful with lemon or vanilla cake, but it also pairs extremely well with chocolate cake, a combination that is very popular at the shops. You can flavour this Swiss meringue buttercream base with either homemade raspberry purée or a purchased variety.

4 large egg whites (½ cup)

1 cup granulated sugar

1 pound unsalted butter, cut into 1-inch cubes, room temperature

⅓ cup Raspberry Purée (page 245, or use store-bought)

1 teaspoon pure vanilla extract

Tip

Store-bought fruit purées can be excellent and save precious time. Just be sure to check the ingredients for no added water and little if any added sugar.

1. In a medium saucepan, bring an inch or so of water to a simmer.

2. In a large heatproof bowl, combine the egg whites and sugar. Place over the simmering water and whisk gently until very hot to the touch or a candy thermometer reads 140°F. Immediately pour the egg white mixture into the bowl of a stand mixer fitted with the whisk attachment.

3. Whisk on medium-high speed until the egg whites have cooled to room temperature, doubled in volume and hold medium peaks, 8 to 10 minutes.

4. Turn the mixer to medium-low speed and slowly add the butter a few cubes at a time, increasing the speed to medium-high after each addition and beating until the butter is fully incorporated before adding more. Once all the butter has been added, continue to beat on medium-high until the buttercream is light and fluffy, 1 to 2 minutes. Stop the mixer to scrape down the sides of the bowl, making sure to scrape the bottom as well.

5. Add the raspberry purée and vanilla. Start the mixer on medium-low speed and gradually increase the speed to medium-high, then beat for 2 minutes.

6. Use immediately or store in an airtight container in the fridge for up to 1 week. Bring buttercream to room temperature before using. Any leftovers may be frozen for up to 3 months.

Recipe is naturally gluten-free.

CLASSIC VANILLA FROSTING

This vanilla frosting is thick enough to pipe easily and retain its shape. The butter and cream balance out the typically overpowering sweetness associated with frostings. We recommend blending it long enough to achieve a creamy smooth texture and to avoid any graininess from the sugar.

3¾ cups icing sugar, sifted

¼ teaspoon salt

¼ cup 35% cream

1 tablespoon pure vanilla extract

1 cup unsalted butter, room temperature

Tip

Because this frosting is white, it takes food colouring very well, particularly if you're looking to achieve soft, delicate pastels.

1. In a medium bowl, whisk together the icing sugar and salt. In a measuring cup, combine the cream and vanilla.

2. In the bowl of a stand mixer fitted with the paddle attachment, cream the butter on medium-high speed until light and fluffy, about 3 minutes. Reduce the speed to medium and alternate adding the icing sugar mixture in 3 additions and the cream in 2 additions, beginning and ending with the sugar mixture. Beat after each addition until fully incorporated, stopping the mixer to scrape down the sides of the bowl when needed. Increase the speed to high and beat for 2 more minutes.

3. Use immediately or store in an airtight container in the fridge for up to 1 week.

Recipe is naturally gluten-free.

**MAKES ENOUGH TO FROST 12 CUPCAKES;
DOUBLE THE RECIPE TO FILL AND MASK A 9-INCH ROUND THREE-LAYER CAKE**

Let's face it, a little alcohol makes everything taste better. Whether it's a touch of Grand Marnier, a hint of Baileys or, in this case, a splash of sparkling wine, the power of alcohol to elevate a dessert is without question. So many cupcakes are kid centred that we thought it would be fun to make a topping with adults in mind.

3¾ cups icing sugar

¼ teaspoon salt

¼ cup 35% cream

1 tablespoon pure vanilla extract

1 cup unsalted butter, room temperature

8 drops red food colouring

Prosecco to taste

Tip

Different types of champagne and sparkling wine have different flavours. We like the flavour of a dry Prosecco in this frosting, but any sparkling wine may be used.

1. In a medium bowl, whisk together the icing sugar and salt. In a measuring cup, combine the cream and vanilla.

2. In the bowl of a stand mixer fitted with the paddle attachment, cream the butter on medium-high speed until light and fluffy, about 3 minutes. Reduce the speed to medium and alternate adding the icing sugar mixture in 3 additions and the cream in 2 additions, beginning and ending with the sugar mixture. Beat after each addition until fully incorporated, stopping the mixer to scrape down the sides of the bowl when needed. Add the red food colouring and Prosecco and beat on high speed for 2 more minutes.

3. Use immediately or store in an airtight container in the fridge for up to 1 week.

Recipe is naturally gluten-free.

DARK CHOCOLATE FUDGE FROSTING

DARK CHOCOLATE
FUDGE FROSTING

MAKES ENOUGH TO FROST 12 TO 15 CUPCAKES OR FILL THE INNER LAYERS OF A 9-INCH ROUND THREE-LAYER CAKE; DOUBLE THE RECIPE TO FILL AND MASK A 9-INCH ROUND THREE-LAYER CAKE

We love a fudge frosting that is very rich and full of chocolate flavour. We recommend using an extra-dark cocoa to significantly boost the flavour. Traditional supermarket cocoa will work too, but it can be bitter, so be sure to taste the frosting frequently as you add it until you achieve the level of chocolate you desire.

4¼ cups icing sugar, sifted

1¾ cups cocoa powder

Rounded ¼ teaspoon salt

1 cup unsalted butter, room temperature

1 cup whole milk, room temperature

Tip

Frostings tend to form a crust soon after they're piped, so if you are using any additional garnishes, be sure to put them in place as soon as you have frosted your cake or cupcakes.

1. In a medium bowl, whisk together the icing sugar, cocoa powder and salt.

2. In the bowl of a stand mixer fitted with the paddle attachment, cream the butter on medium-high speed until light and fluffy, about 3 minutes. Reduce the speed to medium-low and alternate adding the icing sugar mixture in 3 additions and the milk in 2 additions, beginning and ending with the sugar mixture. Beat after each addition until fully incorporated, stopping the mixer to scrape down the sides of the bowl when needed. Increase the speed to high and beat for 3 more minutes.

3. Use immediately or store in an airtight container in the fridge for up to 1 week.

   Recipe is naturally gluten-free.

CARAMEL FROSTING

There are barely words to describe how delicious this frosting is. Brown sugar provides a subtle undertone of maple, and cooking the sugar gives a caramel flavour. Our store manager, Anne-Sophie, says that this frosting reminds her of sucre à la crème from Quebec.

²⁄₃ cup unsalted butter

1¼ cups packed brown sugar

½ cup 35% cream

½ teaspoon salt

2½ cups icing sugar, sifted

Tip

In recipes that call for salt as a garnish or where an enhanced salt flavour is desired, we always prefer to use high-quality fleur de sel rather than regular table salt. The taste is subtler and so there is less chance of overdoing it.

1. Melt the butter in a small saucepan over medium heat. Add the brown sugar, cream and salt, then bring to a boil, stirring constantly. Cook for 3 minutes. Transfer the mixture to a large bowl and allow to cool for about 15 minutes.

2. Using a handheld electric mixer on medium speed, beat in the icing sugar a little at a time until you reach the desired consistency. Add more salt if the frosting tastes too sweet.

3. Use immediately or store in an airtight container in the fridge for up to 1 week.

   Recipe is naturally gluten-free.

PEANUT BUTTER
FROSTING

You could use an all-natural peanut butter in this recipe, but we prefer classic Kraft brand because of its silky smooth texture. This is an addictive frosting that pairs well with chocolate cake, but we also have customers who love it on our chocolate chip banana cake.

3⅓ cups icing sugar, sifted

⅛ teaspoon salt

2 tablespoons + 1½ teaspoons 35% cream

2½ teaspoons pure vanilla extract

1 cup unsalted butter, room temperature

½ cup smooth peanut butter

Tip

Adjust the amount of peanut butter to suit your own palate. It is quite stable, so there is no worry about weakening the structure of the frosting.

1. In a medium bowl, whisk together the icing sugar and salt. In a small bowl, combine the cream and vanilla.

2. In the bowl of a stand mixer fitted with the paddle attachment, cream the butter and peanut butter on medium-high speed until light and fluffy, about 3 minutes. Reduce the speed to medium and alternate adding the icing sugar mixture in 3 additions and the cream in 2 additions, beginning and ending with the sugar mixture. Beat after each addition until fully incorporated, stopping the mixer to scrape down the sides of the bowl when needed. Increase the speed to high and beat for 2 more minutes.

3. Use immediately or store in an airtight container in the fridge for up to 1 week.

   Recipe is naturally gluten-free.

**MAKES ENOUGH TO FROST 12 TO 15 CUPCAKES;
DOUBLE THE RECIPE TO FILL AND MASK A 9-INCH ROUND THREE-LAYER CAKE**

This frosting is thick and rich, but the mint makes it cool and refreshing as well. We like to pair it with our Double Chocolate Cupcakes (page 64), but it would be equally good as a topping, instead of chocolate glaze, on Death by Chocolate Brownies (page 50).

3⅓ cups icing sugar, sifted

⅛ teaspoon salt

2 tablespoons + 1½ teaspoons 35% cream

2½ teaspoons pure vanilla extract

1 teaspoon pure mint extract

15 drops green food colouring

1 cup unsalted butter, room temperature

Tip

Garnish seasonally with crushed candy cane pieces.

1. In a medium bowl, whisk together the icing sugar and salt. In a small bowl, combine the cream, vanilla, mint extract and food colouring.

2. In the bowl of a stand mixer fitted with the paddle attachment, cream the butter on medium-high speed until light and fluffy, about 3 minutes. Reduce the speed to medium and alternate adding the icing sugar mixture in 2 additions and the cream mixture in 1 addition, beginning and ending with the sugar mixture. Beat after each addition until fully incorporated, stopping the mixer to scrape down the sides of the bowl when needed. Increase the speed to high and beat for 2 more minutes.

3. Use immediately or store in an airtight container in the fridge for up to 1 week.

   Recipe is naturally gluten-free.

**MAKES ENOUGH TO FROST 12 TO 15 CUPCAKES;
DOUBLE THE RECIPE TO FILL AND MASK A 9-INCH ROUND THREE-LAYER CAKE**

Much as cream cheese adds a tangy and rich flavour to frostings and buttercreams, the sour cream in this frosting provides a similar flavour but is also slightly tart and sour. This frosting pairs particularly well with hearty cakes like our Classic Hummingbird Cupcakes (page 78), "No Raisin" Carrot Cake (page 90) or Caramel Apple Cake (page 92). It's sure to become a favourite.

½ cup sour cream

½ cup + 3 tablespoons unsalted butter, cool room temperature

2 teaspoons fresh lemon juice

1 teaspoon pure vanilla extract

½ teaspoon salt

4¼ cups icing sugar, sifted

Tip

For a firmer icing texture that is easier to pipe and has more stability, make sure the butter and sour cream are slightly cool.

Sifting your icing sugar beforehand ensures you will have a smooth icing with no lumps or clumps in it.

1. Line a sieve with cheesecloth and set it over a bowl. Put the sour cream in the sieve and let it drain in the fridge overnight. Bring almost to room temperature before using.

2. In the bowl of a stand mixer fitted with the paddle attachment, cream the butter on medium-high speed until light and fluffy, about 3 minutes. Stop the mixer to scrape down the sides of the bowl, then add the drained sour cream. Beat on medium-high speed until smooth. Add the lemon juice, vanilla and salt and beat until well combined.

3. With the mixer on medium-low speed, add the icing sugar, 1 cup at a time, beating after each addition until fully incorporated. Stop the mixer to scrape down the sides of the bowl after each addition.

4. Use immediately or store in an airtight container in the fridge for up to 5 days. Before using, beat the icing in an electric mixer until light and fluffy.

Recipe is naturally gluten-free.

COOKED CREAM CHEESE FROSTING

For years we tried every method possible to make a stable cream cheese frosting that could be kept at room temperature for several hours without losing stability. It wasn't until reading some reference materials about French icings that we learned about roux icing. This boiled icing is nothing short of amazing. It is stable and tastes delicious. We feel as though we have inadvertently stumbled upon the holy grail of frostings, or at the very least a unicorn. It can be tricky to make at first, but be patient and keep trying. The result is definitely worth it.

1 cup granulated sugar

¼ cup all-purpose flour

3 tablespoons cornstarch

¼ teaspoon salt

1½ cups whole milk

4½ teaspoons fresh lemon juice

2 teaspoons pure vanilla extract

1 package (250 g) cream cheese, cut into 1-tablespoon cubes, room temperature

1 cup unsalted butter, cut into 1-tablespoon cubes, room temperature

Tip

Be sure that the butter and cream cheese are not cold or they won't properly incorporate into the cooked flour mixture and lumps of each will remain.

1. In a medium saucepan, combine the sugar, flour, cornstarch and salt. Whisk in the milk a little at a time, making sure no lumps form. Cook over medium heat, whisking constantly, until the mixture thickens to a paste, about 5 minutes. Be sure to cook long enough or the frosting will have a starchy taste.

2. Press the flour mixture through a fine-mesh sieve into a bowl. Place plastic wrap directly on the surface of the mixture to prevent a skin from forming and refrigerate until completely cooled, about 1 hour.

3. Transfer the flour mixture to the bowl of a stand mixer fitted with the whisk attachment and add the lemon juice and vanilla. Whisk on high speed until incorporated and the mixture has loosened a bit.

4. With the mixer on medium-high speed, whisk in the cream cheese 1 cube at a time, making sure each piece is fully incorporated before adding more. Whisk in the butter a cube at a time, again making sure each piece is fully incorporated before adding more. You do not want any visible lumps of cream cheese or butter. Stop to scrape down the sides of the bowl as needed.

5. Once the cream cheese and butter are both added, whisk a little longer until the icing is light and fluffy. Cover the bowl with plastic wrap and refrigerate for 1 hour to allow the icing to firm up before using.

6. Use immediately or store in an airtight container in the fridge for up to 1 week. Before using, fluff the icing with a rubber spatula to stir it and remove any air bubbles.

MAKES ENOUGH TO MASK A 9-INCH ROUND THREE-LAYER CAKE

We love the glossy, light as air appearance of a 7-minute frosting. This classic is easy to make. It's essentially a meringue, but adding corn syrup gives it elasticity and body that makes it great for masking the outside of cakes.

6 large egg whites (¾ cup)

1½ cups granulated sugar

¼ cup water

2 tablespoons corn syrup

1 teaspoon pure vanilla extract

Tip

Because this is a type of meringue, you can toast it with a kitchen blowtorch for a different look and flavour. This frosting sets up immediately, so it is best applied in a more rustic style as it does not remain workable for long.

1. In a medium saucepan, bring an inch or so of water to a simmer.

2. In the bowl of a stand mixer, combine the egg whites, sugar, water and corn syrup. Place over the simmering water and whisk gently and continuously until the sugar has dissolved and a candy thermometer reads 160°F. (If you don't have a candy thermometer, note when the mixture becomes hot to the touch and continue whisking for another minute.)

3. Place the bowl on the mixer and fit it with the whisk attachment. Beat on high speed until the frosting is glossy and holds stiff peaks, about 5 minutes. Beat in the vanilla.

4. Use immediately. Meringues set up quickly and so cannot be stored for future use.

Recipe is naturally gluten-free.

Recipe is naturally dairy-free.

ROYAL ICING

MAKES 4 CUPS

Royal icing is very simple to make and dries hard, which makes it perfect for dipping cookies and piping decorations. The egg whites make the icing slightly elastic, which allows for precision piping. Start out piping simple designs using a larger piping tip, but feel free to experiment with a smaller tip and more elaborate designs as you get comfortable.

4 cups icing sugar

4 large egg whites (½ cup)

Tip

If you are using the royal icing immediately, keep it covered in the mixing bowl, and place it back on to mix for a minute anytime it starts to appear spongy, typically every hour or so. If you have stored it for future use, be sure to beat thoroughly by hand or place it back on the mixer and mix for a minute before using.

1. Sift the icing sugar into the bowl of a stand mixer.

2. Place the bowl on the mixer and fit it with the paddle attachment. With the mixer on low speed, add 2 of the egg whites. Increase the speed to medium-low and mix until combined. Add the remaining 2 egg whites and mix on medium speed for 10 minutes, stopping to scrape down the sides of the bowl at least once.

3. Cover the bowl with plastic wrap or transfer to an airtight container. The royal icing will keep in the fridge for up to 2 days. Before using, bring to room temperature and then beat.

ROYAL ICING FLOOD FOR COOKIES

To make the royal icing a suitable consistency for dipping sugar cookies, water has to be added.

1. In order to dip the tops of the cookies and achieve a smooth surface, water has to be added to the Royal Icing (above) to create a "flood" consistency. Add water 1 teaspoon at a time, stirring after each addition until well combined. The royal icing will have reached the flood stage when, if you lift some with a spoon and drizzle it back into the bowl, it smooths out in 8 to 10 seconds. You want the icing to be thin enough that it will even out once dipped, but thick enough that it will hold its shape and not run off the sides of the cookie as it dries.

2. Hold a cookie upside down and dip the top, but not the sides, in the icing. Pull it out and hold it over the bowl, still upside down, for about 5 sections so that any excess can drip off. Turn the cookie upright and place it on a wire rack or clean baking sheet to dry. Repeat with the remaining cookies. Set them aside for a full 24 hours to dry. If it is not very humid, it may only take 12 hours. Royal icing dries to a very hard consistency, so it is easy to tell when they are ready. The decorated cookies can be stored in an airtight container for up to 1 month.

Recipe is naturally gluten-free.

Recipe is naturally dairy-free.

CHOCOLATE GLAZE

MAKES ABOUT 1 CUP

For years we sold a cake at Bobbette & Belle that was entirely coated in liquid chocolate ganache. It was delicious, but we lived in fear of it cracking in the fridge. After much testing we came up with this glaze, which packs the same chocolate punch as the ganache but is much more stable and forgiving of temperature changes. The corn syrup helps it to stay glossy and uncracked.

½ pound dark chocolate, chopped (about 1¼ cups)

⅔ cup unsalted butter, cut into small pieces, room temperature

1¼ teaspoons corn syrup

½ teaspoon pure vanilla extract

¼ teaspoon fleur de sel (or ⅛ teaspoon table salt)

Tip

If you would like the glaze to be smooth, use it while it is still a touch warm and runny. If you prefer to spread it like a frosting, let it thicken by allowing it to cool fully to room temperature.

1. In a medium saucepan, bring an inch or so of water to a simmer.

2. Combine the chocolate, butter, corn syrup, vanilla and fleur de sel in a large heatproof bowl and set the bowl over the simmering water. Gently and continuously stir until the chocolate and butter are melted and the glaze is smooth. Remove the bowl from the pot and allow the glaze to cool to room temperature.

3. Use immediately or store in an airtight container at room temperature for up to 1 week.

Recipe is naturally gluten-free.

CREAM CHEESE GLAZE

MAKES 1⅓ CUPS

We've included recipes for cream cheese frosting and cream cheese buttercream, but sometimes you simply must have a cream cheese glaze. A glaze in inherently runnier, which makes it perfect for drizzling over our Cinnamon Pull-Apart Bread (page 118) or coating the top of the Holiday Gingerbread Bundt (page 120).

½ cup cream cheese, room temperature

3 tablespoons whole milk

½ teaspoon pure vanilla extract

⅛ teaspoon salt

1½ cups icing sugar, sifted

Tip

Adjust the amount of milk for the desired consistency. More milk will make the glaze more pourable, while less will keep it more like a spreadable icing.

1. In the bowl of a stand mixer fitted with the paddle attachment, combine the cream cheese, milk, vanilla, and salt. Beat on medium-high speed until well blended and there are no visible lumps of cream cheese.

2. Reduce the speed to medium and gradually add the icing sugar, then beat on high speed until completely smooth.

3. Use immediately or store in an airtight container in the fridge for up to 4 days.

Recipe is naturally gluten-free.

MAKES 3 CUPS

Look for a high-quality gianduja chocolate for this ganache. With its nutty flavour and chocolate truffle texture, this ganache works well for filling French macarons and many cakes. It is quite dense, but the milk chocolate component in the gianduja keeps it lighter and creamier than a traditional dark chocolate ganache.

2½ cups gianduja (hazelnut chocolate), finely chopped (14 ounces)

1 cup dark chocolate, finely chopped (7 ounces)

1½ cups 35% cream

Tip

Always keep an eye on the cream while it heats. It can instantaneously go from a bare simmer to what we call "the white volcano."

1. Place the gianduja and dark chocolate in a medium heatproof bowl; set aside. In a small saucepan over medium heat, bring the cream just to a simmer. Pour the hot cream over the chocolate. Wait for 1 minute, then whisk until the chocolate is melted and the mixture is smooth. Allow to cool to room temperature.

2. Use immediately or store in an airtight container in the fridge for up to 1 week.

MASCARPONE CREAM

MAKES 3 ½ CUPS

Mascarpone cheese improves almost any recipe calling for whipping cream. It adds a very subtle yet noticeable flavour. It also gives whipped cream a slightly denser texture, providing a bit of stability.

1½ cups mascarpone cheese

1½ cups 35% cream

½ cup granulated sugar

1½ teaspoons pure vanilla extract

Tip

Try to buy a high-quality mascarpone from a specialty cheese purveyor rather than grocery store brands, which can have a slightly grainy texture.

1. In the bowl of a stand mixer fitted with the whisk attachment, whisk the mascarpone with the cream and sugar until the mixture is thick and increases in volume. Add the vanilla and beat until just combined. Be careful to not overmix or the mixture will take on a curdled appearance.

2. Use the mascarpone cream the same day it is made.

Recipe is naturally gluten-free.

VANILLA PASTRY CREAM

MAKES 2 CUPS

Vanilla pastry cream, or crème pâtissière as it is known in France, is formed by slowly cooking a combination of milk or cream, eggs, sugar, vanilla and cornstarch until the mixture thickens and boils. The resulting consistency is perfect for filling a variety of pastries. It may be used by itself or mixed with whipping cream to achieve a lightened texture that pairs well with desserts like strawberry shortcake.

1¼ cups whole milk

3 large egg yolks

⅓ cup granulated sugar

¼ cup cornstarch

1½ teaspoons pure vanilla extract

1¼ teaspoons unsalted butter, room temperature

⅔ cup 35% cream

Tip

Adding a little butter to pastry cream gives it a smooth, velvety texture.

Do not overwhip your cream, or you will end up with butter!

1. In a small saucepan over medium heat, bring the milk just to a simmer.

2. Meanwhile, in a medium bowl, whisk together the egg yolks, sugar, cornstarch and vanilla until smooth. Slowly pour a thin, steady stream of the hot milk into the egg yolk mixture, whisking all the while. Do not pour the hot milk in all at once or the eggs will scramble.

3. Pour the tempered mixture back into the pot and bring it to a boil over medium heat, whisking constantly. Cook, whisking constantly, until the pastry cream thickens, 1 to 2 minutes.

4. Strain the pastry cream through a fine-mesh sieve into a bowl. (This will remove any egg bits that accidentally cooked too quickly.) Stir in the butter until fully incorporated. Place plastic wrap directly on the surface of the pastry cream to prevent a skin from forming and chill completely in the fridge, 2 to 3 hours. The pastry cream can be stored in the fridge for up to 3 days.

5. Whip the 35% cream until soft peaks form. Gently fold half of the whipped cream into the pastry cream to lighten it. Fold in the remaining whipped cream, being careful not to overmix or the whipped cream will deflate.

Recipe is naturally gluten-free.

MAKES 2 CUPS

Crème anglaise, or pouring custard sauce, is exactly that: a liquid custard that is used as a garnish for all sorts of desserts. It is creamy and rich, has more flavour than whipping cream and isn't as heavy as ice cream. Our Caramel Apple Bread Pudding (page 114) and Quick and Easy Summer Fruit Torte (page 126) would both be delicious served with a little crème anglaise. It is simple to prepare and can be made ahead. You can use vanilla extract in place of the pod, but the small vanilla seeds are quite pleasing.

½ vanilla bean (or 2 teaspoons pure vanilla extract)

1 cup whole milk

1 cup 35% cream

½ cup granulated sugar

6 large egg yolks

Tip

Do not allow the custard to reach a boil or you will scramble the eggs.

Vanilla is the classic flavouring, but you can use others, such as lemon or orange zest, chopped white chocolate, or alcohol like Grand Marnier or dark rum.

1. Split the vanilla bean in half and scrape out the seeds. Place the pod and seeds in a medium saucepan and add the milk, cream and sugar. Bring just to a simmer over medium heat, stirring to dissolve the sugar.

2. Meanwhile, whisk the egg yolks in a medium bowl. Add the hot milk mixture in a thin, steady stream, whisking constantly.

3. Pour the mixture back into the pot and cook over medium heat, stirring constantly with a wooden spoon, until the sauce thickens enough to coat the back of the spoon. Do not let it boil. Strain the sauce through a sieve into a bowl.

4. Serve warm, or place plastic wrap directly on the surface of the custard to prevent a skin from forming and refrigerate until cold. The custard sauce can be kept in an airtight container in the fridge for up to 4 days.

Recipe is naturally gluten-free.

RASPBERRY PURÉE

MAKES ½ CUP, ENOUGH TO FLAVOUR A SINGLE BATCH OF BUTTERCREAM

This is a simple recipe to prepare and results in an intensely flavoured purée. It does not contain much sugar and is therefore quite tart. As such, it is best used to flavour other recipes, but if you'd like to use it as a stand-alone topping, simply increase the sugar to taste.

1 cup frozen raspberries

1 tablespoon granulated sugar

⅓ cup water

1. In a small saucepan, bring the raspberries, sugar and water to a boil over medium-high heat. Cook for 5 minutes, stirring constantly, until the raspberries lose their shape and the mixture thickens slightly.

2. Press the mixture through a fine-mesh sieve into a bowl to remove the seeds. Make sure to scrape vthe outside of the sieve to get all the purée. Allow to cool to room temperature before adding to buttercream. The purée can be stored in an airtight container in the fridge for up to 1 week or may be frozen for up to 3 months.

Recipe is naturally gluten-free.

Recipe is naturally dairy-free.

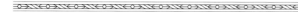

PASSION FRUIT CURD

Many people are only familiar with the traditional lemon curd found in lemon meringue pie, but other tart fruits make lovely curds as well. For us, passion fruit is definitely at the top of that list. Its unique flavour lends a tropical sensibility, which is one of the reasons we pair it with our Coconut Cake with Passion Fruit Curd (page 100).

4 large eggs

2 large egg yolks

1 cup granulated sugar

½ cup passion fruit purée

⅔ cup unsalted butter, cut into 1-inch cubes, room temperature

Tip

Be sure to cook the curd long enough to thicken, but not so long that you scramble the eggs. This recipe does not use gelatin, so the process of slowly cooking the eggs in the curd is what thickens it.

It is important to source a passion fruit purée, not juice, or the curd will be too sweet and lack flavour.

1. In a medium saucepan, bring an inch or so of water to a simmer.

2. In a medium heatproof bowl, whisk together the eggs, egg yolks and sugar until well combined and the mixture has lightened in colour. Slowly pour the passion fruit puree into the egg mixture, whisking constantly while doing so.

3. Place the bowl over the simmering water. Cook the curd, whisking constantly, until it thickens, about 10 minutes. You should be able to dip a spoon into the curd, draw a line through it with a finger and have it hold its shape.

4. Remove the bowl from the pot and whisk in the butter one piece at a time, whisking until each piece is fully incorporated before adding the next.

5. Press the curd through a fine-mesh sieve into a bowl, making sure to scrape the outside of the sieve to get all the curd. Place plastic wrap directly on the surface of the curd to prevent a skin from forming. Place it in the fridge to chill and thicken for 4 to 6 hours.

6. The curd can be stored in the fridge for up to 3 days. Before using, stir with a rubber spatula to loosen it slightly so that it is easier to spread between the layers of cake.

Recipe is naturally gluten-free.

CARAMELIZED HAZELNUTS

MAKES 8 TO 10 CARAMELIZED NUTS

This is a fun and dramatic garnish, but it does require some skill to avoid nasty sugar burns. It is quite quick to pull together once you get the hang of it.

1 cup granulated sugar

2 cups water

8 to 10 whole hazelnuts

1. You will need a foam block and as many toothpicks as you have nuts. Fill a bowl with ice and water; set aside.

2. In a medium saucepan, bring the sugar and water to a boil over medium-high heat. Continue to boil, swirling the pan occasionally to prevent burning, until the sugar starts to caramelize and is amber in colour, 8 to 10 minutes. Do not stir after this point. Periodically wash down the sides of the pot with a clean pastry brush dipped in water to prevent the sugar from crystallizing.

3. Immediately remove from the heat and dip the bottom of the pot in and out of the ice water three or four times to stop the cooking of the caramel but taking care not to cool the caramel so much that it hardens.

4. Use a folded tea towel to prop the pot up on an angle on the counter so that the caramel pools to one side of the pot.

5. Poke a toothpick into each hazelnut, making sure it is securely in place but not pressing too hard or the nut will break in half. Holding the toothpick, dip a hazelnut into the caramel. As you pull the hazelnut out of the caramel, allow a ribbon of caramel to fall back into the pot but adhere to the nut. You may need to dip the nut twice if the caramel coating seems thin and a ribbon does not form. Hold the nut over the pot for a few second to allow the excess caramel to fall back into the pot. The caramel ribbon attached to the nut should harden enough so you can turn the hazelnut right side up and poke the toothpick into the foam.

6. Repeat with the remaining hazelnuts, working as quickly as possible to ensure the caramel does not harden before all the nuts are dipped. If the caramel does harden, return it to the heat to soften slightly. Leave the caramelized hazelnuts poked into the foam until the sugar fully firms up. The caramelized hazelnuts should be used the day they are made.

BULK BARN

www.bulkbarn.ca

Stores located within Canada. No shipping available.

Baking ingredients and specialty ingredients such as chocolate, cocoa, nuts, flavourings, extracts, gelatin, food colouring, cake/cupcake/cookie decorating supplies, spices and candy

CREATIVE BAG

(800) 263-1418 | *www.creativebag.com*

Ships within Canada and USA

Packaging such as boxes and bags for cakes/cupcakes/cookies/confections and other treats

FLOUR CONFECTIONS

(888) 443-2253 | *www.flourconfections.com*

Ships internationally

Specialty ingredients such as chocolate, cocoa, nut flours, flavourings, extracts, gelatin, food colouring, cake/cupcake/cookie decorating supplies, bakeware, baking tools and kitchen appliances

GOLDA'S KITCHEN

(866) 465-3299 | *www.goldaskitchen.com*

Ships internationally

Cookware, bakeware, baking tools, cake/cupcake/cookie decorating supplies and small appliances

KITCHEN STUFF PLUS

(416) 944-2847 x 106 | *www.kitchenstuffplus.com*

Ships within Canada and USA

Cookware, bakeware, baking tools, kitchen utensils and small appliances

LUV2PAK

(888) 588-2725 | *www.luv2pak.com*

Ships within Canada and USA

Packaging such as boxes and bags for cakes/cupcakes/cookies/confections and other treats

MCCALL'S

(800) 541-3415 | *www.mccalls.ca*

Ships internationally

Specialty ingredients such as chocolate, cocoa, nuts, flavourings, extracts, gelatin, food colouring, cake/cupcake/cookie decorating supplies, bakeware, baking tools and small appliances

MICHAELS

(800) 642-4235 | *canada.michaels.com*

Ships within Canada and USA

Cake/cookie/cupcake decorating supplies, bakeware, baking tools, packaging, Wilton products (fondant, food colouring, sprinkles, coating chocolate)

ULINE

(800) 295-5510 | *www.uline.ca*

Ships within Canada and USA

Packaging such as boxes and bags for cakes/cupcakes/cookies/confections and other treats

WILLIAMS-SONOMA

(877) 812-6235 | *www.williams-sonoma.ca*

Ships internationally

Cookware, bakeware, baking tools, kitchen utensils, small appliances and specialty ingredients such as cocoa, flavourings and extracts

WILTON

(888) 373-4588 | *www.wilton.com*

Ships internationally

Cake/cookie/cupcake decorating supplies, bakeware, baking tools, packaging, specialty ingredients such as fondant, food colouring, sprinkles and coating chocolate

VOLUME EQUIVALENTS

TEASPOONS TO ML

⅛ teaspoon	0.5 mL
¼ teaspoon	1 mL
½ teaspoon	2 mL
¾ teaspoon	4 mL
1 teaspoon	5 mL
1 ¼ teaspoons	6 mL
1 ½ teaspoons	7 mL
1 ¾ teaspoons	9 mL
2 teaspoons	10 mL
2 ½ teaspoons	12 mL
2 ¾ teaspoons	14 mL
4 teaspoons	20 mL
4 ½ teaspoons	22 mL

TABLESPOONS TO ML

1 tablespoon	15 mL
2 tablespoons	30 mL
3 tablespoons	45 mL
5 tablespoons	75 mL
6 tablespoons	90 mL

CUPS TO ML

¼ cup	60 mL
⅓ cup	75 mL
½ cup	125 mL
⅔ cup	150 mL
¾ cup	175 mL
1 cup	250 mL
1 ¼ cups	300 mL
1 ⅓ cups	325 mL
1 ½ cups	375 mL
1 ⅔ cups	400 mL
1 ¾ cups	425 mL
2 cups	500 mL
2 ¼ cups	550 mL
2 ⅓ cups	575 mL
2 ½ cups	625 mL
2 ⅔ cups	650 mL
2 ¾ cups	675 mL
3 cups	750 mL
3 ⅓ cups	825 mL
3 ½ cups	875 mL
3 ⅔ cups	900 mL
3 ¾ cups	925 mL
4 cups	1 L
4 ½ cups	1.1 L
5 cups	1.25 L
6 cups	1.5 L
8 cups	2 L

WEIGHT EQUIVALENTS

OUNCES TO GRAMS

½ ounce	14 g
1 ounce	28 g
1 ½ ounces	42 g
2 ounces	55 g
3 ounces	85 g
3 ½ ounces	100 g
4 ounces	115 g
5 ounces	140 g
6 ounces	170 g
7 ounces	200 g
8 ounce	225 g
9 ounces	250 g
10 ounces	285 g
⅔ pound	300 g
12 ounces	340 g
14 ounces	400 g
1 pound	450 g

LENGTH EQUIVALENTS

INCHES TO CM

⅛ inch	3 mm
¼ inch	5 mm
⅓ inch	8 mm
⅜ inch	9 mm
½ inch	1 cm
¾ inch	2 cm
1 inch	2.5 cm
1 ½ inches	4 cm
2 inches	5 cm
2 ½ inches	6 cm
3 inches	8 cm
4 ½ inches	11 cm
5 inches	12 cm
6 inches	15 cm
8 inches	20 cm
9 inches	23 cm
10 inches	25 cm
11 inches	28 cm
13 inches	34 cm
14 inches	35 cm
15 inches	38 cm
20 inches	50 cm